BLOODY BRITISH HISTORY

HISTORY

PLYMOUTH

LAURA QUIGLEY

The
History
Press

To Ian
A 'Desert Rat' who survived the horrors of war,
never to speak of them.

The History Press
The Mill, Brimscombe Port
Stroud, Gloucestershire, GL5 2QG
www.thehistorypress.co.uk

British Library Cataloguing in Publication Data.
A catalogue record for this book is available from the British Library.

ISBN 978 0 7524 6638 5

Typesetting and origination by The History Press
Printed and bound in Great Britain by
Marston Book Services Limited, Oxfordshire

CONTENTS

NOTES AND ACKNOWLEDGEMENTS

GATHERING THESE STORIES has been a marvellous adventure. Plymouth has had more than its fair share of 'horrible history' and it was a difficult task selecting just which ghastly and incredible stories to choose. Sadly, this also meant leaving out some of my favourites – there was certainly enough for a second volume (hint to my editor there!). So this is by no means a complete history of Plymouth, and I recommend looking through the bibliography for some further terrific stories. All mistakes in re-telling these grisly tales are, of course, completely my own.

I include some individuals born in Plymouth who had grisly adventures elsewhere and I have used the modern Plymouth boundaries to define the area, incorporating the old towns of East Stonehouse, Dock (now known as Devonport), Stoke Damerel, Tamerton, Plympton and Plymstock, and also Cawsand. Although Cawsand is on the south west of Plymouth Sound and officially in Cornwall, to write about the customs officers of Plymouth and not mention their tormenting adversaries the Cawsand smugglers would be like writing about Normans and not mentioning the Saxons, so the rebellious 'free traders' of Cawsand must also take their place in Plymouth's history.

Huge thanks to everyone who read my first book, *The Devil Comes to Dartmoor*; your support, encouragement and reviews were just wonderful. I am very grateful to my parents in particular, who seem to have bought copies for all of their friends! Thanks also to everyone at The History Press for their help, especially Cate, Declan, Ross and Ian who put up with all my emails. Marketing the first book while writing the second was quite a learning curve for me! Check out Facebook and www.lauraquigley.moonfruit.com for news and more images. I hope you find the following stories as darkly entertaining as I do.

Thanks also to the Thomas Fisher Rare Books Library, University of Toronto, for kind permission to use their images.

BLOODY BRITISH HISTORY

PLYMOUTH

Guildhall Square in the early 1900s, before it was destroyed during the Second World War.

8,000 BC

THE END OF THE WORLD

PLYMOUTH WAS BORN at the end of the world. More than 10,000 years ago, there was no deep Plymouth harbour, and no English Channel. The Ice Age had drawn the seas away, leaving miles of tundra and grasslands in a vast river valley that divided the land masses we now think of as Britain and Europe. North Devon was under the ice. Rivers that would shape Plymouth harbour were then merely tributaries, digging out the cliffs as they flowed south into the fertile valley and joined the river into the Atlantic Ocean.

The valley was populated by nomadic hunter-gatherers, who moved north to hunt on the great tundra that was Dartmoor. They then returned south each year with the onset of winter. They made their homes on the freezing northern frontiers. These first Plymothians were a hard people: resilient, ferocious hunters. Once they had chased lions and hyenas in southern Britain, but now, with the coming of the Ice Age, they hunted mammoth and woolly rhinoceros, bears, wolves and reindeer. They travelled in canoes to trade

their wares with Europe. One family made a home in the caves around Cattedown, with spectacular views of the 'English Channel' valley.

Around 10,000 years ago, the Ice Age ended and the climate slowly changed. Sea levels rose again, steadily at first. A new sea formed – the North Sea far to the north-east of Britain, its waters lapping against a natural dam formed by a series of ridges somewhere between Dover and Calais. The early hunters moved their settlements to new coastlines. With a warmer, wetter climate, the scrublands surrounding Britain became woodlands. The family at Cattedown now hunted smaller game amidst the forests of birch and pine, and gathered nuts, eggs and shellfish. They adapted, survived and thrived.

But they could not foresee the end of the world.

Around 5500 BC, the seas suddenly rose again. Some say Norwegian glacial lakes burst their banks and flooded south. The natural dam near Dover collapsed under the weight of water and the North Sea erupted into the valley below. A tsunami

A vision of the prehistoric coastline.
(Bart Hickman, SXC)

of unimaginable proportions engulfed southern Britain. The torrent destroyed everything in its path, flooding the valley and forming the English Channel. A forest at Bovisand, near Plymouth, drowned. The swirling maelstrom of water battered the steep hills, carving out a new coastline and forming estuaries around the rivers Plym and Tamar.

And so Plymouth was born, in the midst of devastation, eventually to become one of the most famous deep-water harbours in the world.

To the human population of the time, it was a catastrophe. Hundreds if not thousands died – a whole society living in the 'English Channel' valley drowned, their river settlements submerged and their remains swept away into the deep Atlantic Ocean.

What of the hunter-gatherer family who for so many generations had made their home in Cattedown? In 1886 a local journalist and antiquarian called R.N. Worth discovered caves in Cattedown, which is now a headland between the river Plym and the harbour. The caves contained the remains of fifteen Homo sapiens that were around 5,000 years old, along with the bones of hyenas, wolves, deer, mammoth and woolly rhinoceros which were up to 30,000 years old. Sadly these remains, once kept safely at the Athenaeum in Plymouth, were all but destroyed in another period of devastation for Plymouth – the Blitz of the Second World War – though the few charred pieces that survived are now on display at the Plymouth City Museum and Art Gallery at North Hill. It is astonishing to imagine what the remaining skull there in its glass case in the museum must be thinking – to have survived millennia, an Ice Age and a deluge, only to be bombed by the Germans.

No one will ever be certain what actually happened to these fifteen people in Cattedown. Perhaps they were drowned as they slept. Perhaps they survived the deluge, living on the high ground, and were buried in their time on the shores of the old world. For many years after the deluge, ancient man would ride out into the Channel in small boats to drop tributes into the water – a memorial to their ancestors and an old world they would never see again.

As the few survivors stood on the new coastline, they knew their world had ended. Gazing out over a vast new sea, they realised that to trade or even to communicate with the rest of the known world, they were going to need bigger boats.

According to legend, two giants once fought a bloody battle to the death on Plymouth Hoe, a battle that would determine the future of England. The first giant was called Gogmagog, 20ft tall, leader of the native giants, defending his Stone Age homeland against the invading Britons. The second was Corineus, 7ft tall, a chief among the Bronze Age invaders.

The day before, Gogmagog's men had launched a sudden and murderous assault on the invaders, ripping them to pieces with their bare hands. Recovering from their initial shock, the surviving Britons rallied and used their superior agility and weaponry to wipe out the marauding giants, leaving only Gogmagog alive, wounded and in chains. They dragged the fallen Gogmagog to Plymouth Hoe, where Corineus challenged Gogmagog to a fight to the death. The Britons' champion lifted Gogmagog onto his shoulders and, taking a few last heavy steps to the cliff, hurled the giant over into the water, where his body was dashed and broken on the rocks below.

It is the blood of the giant, it is said, that made the rocks around Plymouth turn red. In medieval times, two giant figures called Gog and Gogmagog were carved into the chalk on Plymouth Hoe, and they remained there for centuries, tended by the city's council, until the building of the Citadel on that site in the late 1600s. During the excavation for the Citadel's foundations a huge jawbone and teeth were discovered, of a size that suggested that they could only have belonged to a giant…

Trojans cremating their dead: according to the legend, the first Britons were Trojan exiles attacked by stone age Plymothian giants. (With the kind permission of the Thomas Fisher Rare Book Library, University of Toronto)

THE STONE HOUSE

WHEN THE SAXONS invaded the South West of England, sometime in the late seventh century, they discovered a ruined stone house on the shores of Plymouth Sound, on the edges of the salt marshes that once infested that area.

In 1882 a strange stone building was re-discovered during engineering works to raise Stonehouse Bridge, near Newport Street. The ancient building comprised a series of rectangular chambers or crypts, each containing the burnt remains of

Stonehouse Bridge today, where the Roman remains were found during engineering work.

───── ⬥⬥⬥ ─────

In AD 997, Vikings successfully raided Plymouth, stealing precious metals and coin, attacking all who stood in their path. They anchored in Barn Pool, near Mount Edgcumbe, then sailed up the Tamar River systems and ransacked the Anglo-Saxon mint at Lydford, burning, pillaging and slaying. Ordulf's Minster at Tavistock was burned to the ground before the Vikings made their daring escape. Previously the Vikings had joined the Cornish Celts in the west to attack the Saxon forces in Devon. The victorious Saxons subsequently established the east bank of the Tamar River as the border dividing the Saxons and the Celtic Cornish. The two populations once lived and worked together throughout the south-west peninsula, but the Vikings tore them apart.

───── ⬥⬥⬥ ─────

Skeleton of a Viking ship.
(Melanie Kuipers, SXC)

human bodies. The stone house was likely to have been a Roman crematorium.

Evidence of Roman settlement in Plymouth is sparse. A hoard of Roman coins was found in 1894, probably the pay for soldiers, while small artefacts have been discovered all around the Plymouth Sound, at Plymstock, Mount Batten, Millbay and Sutton Pool, including a small statue of Mercury, the god of trade. What evidence there is suggests a small Roman outpost, administering Celtic tin and copper production. The South West was very muddy back then, and the Romans were renowned for their aversion to mud, so they didn't venture much past Exeter if they could help it.

Rome fell and the Saxons arrived in Plymouth to discover the strange house made of stone. The Romans built their crematoria like Roman villas – literally a house of the dead built beyond the walls of their settlements. The Saxons found the ruined Roman house of the dead on the edge of the marsh very ominous indeed, a morbid fascination that ultimately led to the founding of the village named Stonehouse on the shores of Plymouth Sound.

Stonehouse is closely associated with the word Cremyll, with Cremyll Street leading towards Devil's Point headland, and the opposite headland called Cremyll (sometimes pronounced 'crimble', though the origins of the name are obscure). *Cremare* is the Latin for 'to burn up'; perhaps the grisly crematorium inspired the name?

A burial mound from the Bronze Age was discovered in Mount Edgcumbe Country Park, dating back to 1200 BC, obviously the burial site of someone very important. Bronze mirrors, daggers and coins have been discovered on the opposite headland, at Mount Batten, suggesting a long period of Bronze Age settlement.

Plymouth from Mount Edgcumbe. (Courtesy of the Library of Congress, LC-DIG-ppmsc-08784)

THE BLACK DEATH AND OTHER AILMENTS

IN 1066 THE Normans conquered England and all the Saxon manors around Plymouth changed hands – at the point of a sword. The Norman Barons viciously suppressed a Saxon rebellion, and then established a line of great stone castles along the South West peninsula to control the Saxon population. The Saxons had already established a range of south-facing defences around Plymouth harbour to repel any raids from the sea, extending the previous fortifications of the Britons, the Celts and the Romans. However, the Normans confused the local Saxon lookouts by attacking by land – a cry of 'they're behind you!' might have changed the course of history – and the Normans besieged Exeter before conquering all the lands around Plymouth.

The name Plymouth was then unknown, with Sutton Pool (or South Town Pool) just a small fishing village. The main settlement was then at Plympton, where the Saxons' Priory governed all tin mining and local administration, and it was probably this 'plym-town' that gave the nearby river its name (rather than the other way around).

Observing the substantial wealth of Plympton Priory, the Norman Baron Baldwin de Redvers built his formidable Plympton Castle right next door. His soldiers kept hot oil and coal ready on the castle's battlements to be hurled down on any rebellious Saxon monks, and so Plymouth fell under the absolute control of the Normans.

Some years later, Baron Baldwin de Redvers made the mistake of supporting Empress Matilda in her battle with her cousin King Stephen over the English throne, and in retaliation King Stephen razed Baldwin de Redvers' fine castle to the ground. With de Redvers out of the way, another Norman family – the Valletorts, based at Tremarton Castle on the other side of the Tamar – moved in to claim the land around Sutton, which infuriated the monks at Plympton Priory. The Priory's nearest waterways were silting up with the effluence from tin mining, so the ships chose instead to anchor in Sutton Pool to load their valuable cargoes, and the income to Plympton Priory suffered. Many years were spent arguing with the Valletorts over

Beggars were driven out of Plymouth in this era. (With the kind permission of the Thomas Fisher Rare Book Library, University of Toronto)

the growing settlement around Sutton Pool and the influential port that would become Plymouth.

In 1254 the little village of Plymouth was finally awarded market status, which brought with it ownership of a ducking stool and a pillory, providing the people with centuries of entertainment. (Along with 'bull baiting' under the Hoe.) In 1498 Harry Hornebroke was paid to make a new pillory, and others paid to secure and whip the pilloried prisoners. Crowds could enjoy pelting the prisoners with rotten vegetables. The pillory was still in use as late as 1813, this time to punish a husband and his wife for offending public morals.

The laws in the new town were often cruel. Beggars and the mad were literally beaten out of Plymouth. In 1568 a man called Robert Cottell was paid good wages to do just that, while suspected whores were whipped and exiled. However, life wasn't much better for those permitted to live in Plymouth. The busy streets were narrow and dirty, with sewage running down the open drains; many houses were overcrowded and in disrepair; and illness was rife and spread quickly.

Leprosy was commonplace, made worse by the unhealthy diet and poor hygiene of the impoverished inhabitants. The illness caused skin sores, muscle weakness and nerve damage, resulting in loss of feeling in the sufferer's hands and feet. In the worst cases, the patient became horribly disfigured. Leper houses – or Maudlyn houses – were established in Plympton in 1307, and also in North Hill to quarantine the patients. Not all the patients actually had leprosy. Anyone with anything contagious or incurable, including mental illness, could end up in one of these leper houses, living on charity. In 1590 a man called Edwards was paid to carry a woman 'distracted of her wits' to the Maudlyn house at Plympton.

Then, in 1348, the Black Death arrived. The virulent bubonic plague was carried to Devon on the fleas of black rats. The plague had spread throughout Europe from Asia, and arrived in Weymouth in Dorset in May 1348, carried there by a ship from Gascony. Another ship heading from Weymouth to Bristol then transported the disease around the Devon and Cornish coasts, before it infested Bristol with an epidemic of misery, and the pestilence travelled on inland via the waterways. By August 1348 it had devastated Devon and spread to Cornwall, killing 1,900 in Exeter, 1,500 in Bodmin and half the population of Truro by mid-1349. Half Europe's population – an estimated 25 million people – died in less than two years.

The first signs of the disease were swellings in the armpits and groin, followed by red boils that quickly turned black – the 'buboes' that gave the plague its name. Gangrene soon set in, affecting the lungs and causing incredible pain, often to the point of insanity – maddened victims were reported running through the streets, dispersing the disease. The victims vomited blood, passing the infection on to the next poor unfortunate. Initially the plague spread only through contact with biting fleas or infected victims, but soon it became air-born and just breathing the same air as a sufferer could pass on the horrific symptoms. Attempts were made to quarantine the sick, but many victims were simply abandoned in their homes by terrified relatives and friends. Anyone trying to treat the disease, such as physicians or the clergy, soon joined the dead. The corpses became so many that coffins were replaced by mass graves outside the towns, with parents carrying their dead children to be thrown into the pit, often just before dying themselves.

Treatment seemed impossible. Though they correctly identified that the plague was carried in the air, all they had to protect themselves was the scent of pomanders or herbs. They thought that if they couldn't smell it, they couldn't catch it. Of course, they were wrong. Charlatans sold 'cures', the wealthy buying expensive potions made from gold and pearls in a desperate effort to save themselves, but some of the treatments were as toxic as the illness itself. Many believed the plague to be the wrath of a vengeful God, blaming society's wickedness, immodest clothing or even disobedient children for the onset of the Black Death. The apocalypse was nigh, it seemed. King Edward III pronounced to the bishops:

> For we hope that if, by God's grace, the people drive out this spiritual weakness from their hearts, the malignancy of the air and of the other elements will also depart.

It was all to no avail: the clergy themselves died in ever-increasing numbers. Even the Archbishop of Canterbury perished in 1349. Between January and September 1349, nearly 350 of the clergy in the priories and abbeys of Devon and Cornwall succumbed to the disease. The records specific to Plymouth for 1348 and 1349 have been lost, but in 1349 the Priory at Plympton made a desperate plea to the authorities to permit them to invest underage and illegitimate boys – there were just not enough men left alive in Plymouth to take on the necessary duties at the Priory.

In 1882 Arthur Conan Doyle, later to become famous as the creator of Sherlock Holmes, arrived in Stonehouse as a newly qualified physician to work in the practice of Dr George Budd – a plaque on Durnford Street marks the house. Conan Doyle was rather surprised by Dr Budd's bizarre ideas for curing the sick. On one occasion, a young girl with an irritating cough was placed on the mantelpiece and warned that if she coughed again she would fall into the fire and burn. Dr Budd and Conan Doyle then tried to cure a man with lockjaw by throwing food at each other, thereby making the poor man laugh. Conan Doyle quickly moved to Southsea.

The Black Friars' Distillery, now owned by Plymouth Gin, is said to be haunted. The distillery is all that remains of the Black Friar's Monastery that was near Sutton Pool, and the building was used over the years as a debtors' prison, a refuge for asylum-seeking Huguenots and the last place in England where the pilgrims rested before heading off on the *Mayflower*. Part of the building was also hit by German fire bombs in the Second World War at a time when it was an air-raid shelter. A monk-like figure has been sighted in various rooms, and the ladies' restroom is haunted by a woman who was reportedly stabbed there.

The Black Friars' Distillery, now Plymouth Gin, at the Barbican.

As the Black Death spread from village to village, society fell apart. Livestock roamed free, crops went untended, and people died of starvation as well as disease. Women who survived the plague were often left barren for many years afterwards, too weak to bear children.

Just as the first wave of the epidemic abated, as the population seemed to stabilise and recover, the second and third plagues arrived, perhaps less virulent but seeming to concentrate on the young born since the first plague. In the mid-1300s, entire generations were decimated.

The plague hit Plymouth and the surrounding towns again and again over the centuries. In 1580, 26 shillings was raised in Plymouth to relieve Kingsbridge

people suffering another outbreak. In 1590 four men were paid to keep watch in Plymouth, to maintain the areas of quarantine and ensure local people were kept away from the infected areas, but they seem to have failed in their task – in 1594 Roger Swinsbury, his wife and their two sons all died of the plague. In 1624 houses in Oreston and ships in the harbour were searched for another suspected outbreak, which then hit the prison – the stink of the infected was so horrendous that a man called John Page was paid to scrub the prison clean. Poor John then had the gruesome task of establishing a 'plague house' in the fields just outside Plymouth, to remove the plague victims from the town and into quarantine.

AD 1296-1404

THE BLACK PRINCE AND FRENCH FIRE

WHILE PLYMOUTH WAS suffering outbreaks of plague, it was also under attack from the French.

In the thirteenth and fourteenth centuries, the English Kings still saw France as their ancestral homeland. Having inherited vast lands from the Normans, they owned more of France than the French King. However, the disastrous reign of King John lost them most of their French domain, leaving them with just a few small provinces in Gascony – just enough to cause a lot of trouble.

King Edward I of England retained the title 'Duke of Normandy', but as a Duke he was required to swear fealty to the French King, Philippe IV. The English King refused to bow to the French King. The French King reclaimed Gascony in retaliation. Edward I immediately stopped all passage of ships to the Continent, raising a vicious invading army of felons and criminals, asked to volunteer for paid service in Gascony.

After some false starts due to bad weather, King Edward I assembled a great fleet of 325 ships at Plymouth in January 1296, under the leadership of his brother Edmund. But Edmund sickened and was dead by June, leaving the Earl of Lincoln to lead the attack on French forces mobilising in Gascony. As the fleet sailed, the King and his entourage stayed at Plympton Priory. It was a costly war, ended only by a truce negotiated by the Pope himself, which was then strengthened by a marriage between King Edward's son and King Philippe's fourth child, Isabella.

Battles over the treaty raged on and on, claims and counter-claims going on for years, until the worst possible outcome for the French throne: Philippe IV's eldest sons died, leaving the throne of France in dispute, and Isabella, wife of the now King Edward II, with a rightful claim. (Although the French later passed a law that women could not accede to the French throne, Isabella's son retained a claim, sowing the seeds for the Hundred Years' War between England and France.)

In 1324 Edward II and a younger son of Philippe IV fought a brutal short war in Gascony, and the English forces were decimated. Some say this defeat alone led

Edward I, who stayed at Plympton Priory whilst his troops were attacking France.

therefore did a deal that he would forfeit his claim to the French throne in return for Gascony alone. Philippe VI reneged on the deal and invaded Gascony anyway, and war was declared (again) with open hostilities.

Suddenly French ships were raiding settlements along the Devon and Somerset coasts, and in 1337 all available English forces were put on alert. A series of beacons, fuelled by pitch and manned constantly by five-man crews, were established on all high grounds and headlands to announce the sight of any invading French ships. All coastal cities were frantically fortified, their defences reviewed and strengthened, and all available men conscripted into a militia called the 'Garde de la Mer'.

In 1339 Plymouth was attacked by eighteen French ships and the population fled inland in fear of the French 'pirates'. The invasion was successfully repulsed by forces led by the Earl of Devon, Hugh Courtenay. His forces for the entire Devon coastline consisted of just 175 armed men and 140 archers, but they managed to stave off the French attack. The historian Stowe described the fighting (with spelling amended for clarity):

to King Edward II being deposed by his own wife, Isabella – behind every failed man is a bitter woman! Their son was then crowned King Edward III. In 1328 the last son of Philippe IV died and the French throne passed to a cousin, proclaimed King Philippe VI (with number V already dead!). The English King Edward III retained the stronger claim on the French throne and an overwhelming desire for payback against the French.

However, Gascony was worth a fortune to the English: its wine and salt were exceedingly profitable. King Edward III

At length they entered Plymouth Haven, where they burnt certain great ships and a great part of the town... There they were met by Hugh Courtenay, Earl of Devon, a knight of four-score years. A hand to hand fight followed; many of the pirates were killed, and the residue fled back to their galleys. Not being able to come upon them by wading, many were drowned in the sea to the number of 500; of the townsmen, only 89 were killed. A second attack was repulsed, and the enemy retired to Southampton.

On 1 August 1340 the French attacked Plymouth again. They first burnt Teignmouth, then they assailed Plymouth, but, finding it well-defended, they did little damage – apart from burning some farms and taking a knight prisoner.

In the meantime, King Edward III received news that the French were amassing a fleet of 190 ships to invade England. He launched a pre-emptive strike, which destroyed almost all of the French ships in the Battle of Sluys. The English archers unleashed a torrent of arrows before leaping aboard the French ships and forcing thousands of French soldiers into the sea, where they drowned.

The news of the defeat was allegedly broken to the French King by his jester, who informed the King that the English were cowards. 'How so?' enquired the King. 'Because they have not the courage to leap into the sea, like the French and Normans at Sluys,' he replied. Tens of thousands of French troops were killed, and their bloated corpses would have floated to the surface by the harbour for weeks afterwards. Though Edward III himself was wounded in this battle (hit in the thigh with either an arrow or a crossbow bolt, it is thought), it put an end to the threat of French invasion for some time.

Edward then launched his own counter-invasion in 1346, with Plymouth sending twenty-six ships, manned by 603 men, to join an invading fleet. After capturing Caen, the English forces trounced the French at the Battle of Crecy, largely due to some fortunes in the weather, but mostly due to the power and skill of the English archers. Their 5ft-long yew bows could fire a 3ft arrow with a steel tip able to penetrate a 4in-thick solid oak door. The French relied on their armour for defence, but their armour could not compete against such brutal fire-power.

Edward then besieged Calais, starving the city into submission. After nine months of disrupted food supplies, having been forced to eat rats, the besieged population ejected 500 children and the elderly in a last effort to ensure the survival of the remaining adult men and women. The English refused to help the desperate 500 exiles and merely watched as the old and the young slowly starved to death just outside the town walls.

In time, the fight would be passed on to King Edward III's son, another Edward – better known as the Black Prince – who established his headquarters in Plymouth. In 1348 the Black Prince stayed at Plympton Priory as he prepared his forces for a further invasion of France. However, the Black Death ravaging Devon and France at the time delayed his plans. His father, of course, attributed the spread of the plague to the people's lack of morality, and not the chaos of continuous warfare!

Not until 1356 could the Black Prince again assemble his invasion fleet – a force of 3,000 men gathered in Plymouth town, which then had a population of only around 2,000. Food and supplies were brought to Plymouth from Cornwall, Devon and Somerset and the Sheriffs of Devon and Cornwall were ordered to supply gangways for the ships and hurdles to corral the horses as they fought their way ashore in France.

Despite initial delays, the Black Prince led his forces to victory in the Battle of Poitiers and captured the new French King Jean II, who was brought back to Plymouth a prisoner. The war-ravaged party escorting the tragic figure of the defeated

The Black Prince capturing the King of France.

French monarch on his white horse formed a triumphant procession from Plymouth to Exeter and on to London. Treaties were signed, the French King released, and the Black Prince set up his court at Aquitaine as the French government fell into turmoil. The Treaty of Brétigny in 1360 gave England authority over Aquitaine, half of Brittany, Calais and Ponthieu, though subsequent attempts by the Black Prince to take Paris failed.

The triumph did not last long. In 1372 the King of Castile defeated the English fleet and the English were left with lands only in Calais, Bordeaux and Bayonne. The year before, the Black Prince had returned to Plymouth from failed wars in Spain – he was already a very sick man who would be dead before his father, never to take the throne. Plymouth had played a major role in his triumphs and would mourn his loss. A window in the old Guildhall once celebrated the victories of the Black Prince, but sadly it was destroyed by the bombs of the Second World War.

In 1377 the French attacked again. Edward III and his son were dead, and their successor, King Richard II, was only ten years old. The attacks ravaged Plymouth, leaving it in a state of impoverished decay and ruin, desperate for new defences. The people pleaded to reduce their dues to Plympton Priory in the midst of the devastation. Richard II subsequently assigned monies – from the town's income, of course, not his own – to strengthen its defences and build a wall around the city under the direction of the Priory – but the wall would not be built in time for the next attack.

The Spanish Castilians were also still a threat to the coastal towns. In the 1380s, Richard II worked with his new Portuguese allies to keep the Castilian galleys out of the Channel while his uncle's forces marched through Brittany in a failed effort to deliver it from the French. By 1396 Richard II settled for a peace treaty with the French which seems to have lasted until his successor, King Henry IV, came to the throne in 1399. The following year, Plymouth was again under attack.

In 1400 the French commander John of Bourbon attacked Plymouth, on his return from aiding the Welsh in their bid for independence. Bourbon's fleet chased some trading ships into Plymouth Sound and attacked the town, though this time unsuccessfully. Twelve of Bourbon's ships were sunk in the harbour and he barely managed to escape with his life. Plymouth celebrated the victory, but worse was yet to come.

The attack by the Bretons in 1403 was the most destructive of all the attacks on Plymouth. It is still commemorated by Freedom Fields, a memorial park established in the town following the battle. On the night of 9 August 1403 thirty Breton ships, manned with 1,200 men, under their leader the Sieur du Chastel, sailed into the dark harbour and anchored in the

Cattewater. The Plymouth watch raised the alarm and took their defensive positions. Cannons were dragged to the Hoe and their shot successfully aimed at the Breton ships, but this did not prevent the Bretons travelling further along the Cattewater and landing 1 mile from the town, intending to take Plymouth from the north.

The Bretons plundered and burned 600 wood-built houses on the north-east of Plymouth. Hand-to-hand fighting then broke out in the narrow streets around what is now Exeter Street, but the Plymothians held fast and fought hard against the onslaught of the Breton invaders. Many of du Chastel's men were killed or captured as they tried to fight their way into the city. By 10 a.m. on 10 August, the Bretons were in retreat, fleeing back to their remaining ships, though with plenty of treasure and a few prisoners of their own.

Since that day, an area of Plymouth to the north-east has been known as Breton (or Briton) side, and Freedom Day was celebrated on 10 August for many centuries after. It was a day of carnival in the classic sense, a licence to drink and re-enact the fights and feuds between the Old Town Boys and the Burton (or Breton) Boys. The victors would be awarded a barrel of beer in Freedom Fields, and the ceremonies were held every year until 1792 – when the festivities were curtailed after the revellers

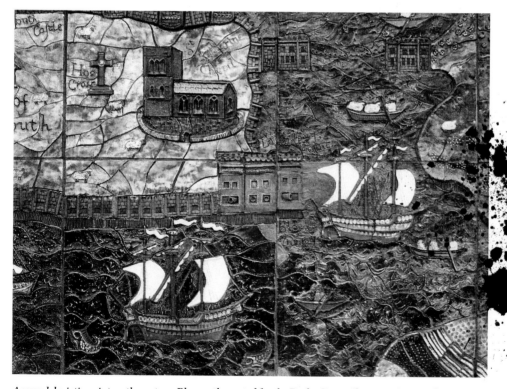

A mural depicting sixteenth-century Plymouth created for the Drake Circus Shopping Centre. The Breton invaders sailed up the Plym River to the east of the harbour, landing at Cattewater, and attacked the old town from the north.

The Cattewater in Plymouth Sound. (With the kind permission of the Thomas Fisher Rare Book Library, University of Toronto)

suffered broken collarbones. However, the carnival continued in its own fashion – in 1809 a blind pugilist still held the title of Burton Chief.

King Henry IV retaliated quickly to avenge the destruction of Plymouth. From Dartmouth in October 1403, he sent the English fleet under the command of William de Wilford to attack Brittany, burning forty ships and seizing 1,000 tons of wine. His forces then laid waste large areas of Penarch and St Mathieu. In 1404 du Chastel was back, this time with the Breton Admiral Jean de Penhors, and the Breton fleet attacked Dartmouth. However, Dartmouth's defences had already been strengthened in preparation for the attack and du Chastel was killed in a hailstorm of arrows. A reported 100 prisoners were taken, including du Chastel's brothers.

Although the Breton Admiral escaped and England would continue to fight over lands in France, including their astounding victory over the French at the Battle of Agincourt in 1415, the Devon coast at last remained free from further French attacks – at least, for the time being...

SCURVY DOGS

THE MODERN IMAGE of English pirates as colourful rogues is far from the truth. Piracy was a profession for bloody-thirsty murderers and thieves, evil marauders intent on destruction and lining their own pockets. Yet some of the worst worked for the government – there was a very fine line between the criminal pirates and the government's paid 'privateers', determined only by who they were attacking at the time.

During the Hundred Years' War, with so many English men fighting in France, Plymouth – like many coastal towns – was overrun by pirates and brigands. While the English forces were raiding French ships in the Channel in acts of war, the pirates were raiding all the other ships in acts of terrorism – the distinction between the two attacks only based on the nationality of the victims. To be fair, the men at sea could not always be expected to distinguish which ships were French, so any foreign ships were seen as the enemy and therefore ripe for plundering.

The first mention of a pirate in Plymouth is Henry Don in 1403. In the midst of the worst French attacks on the town, he was caught thieving and pillaging the wrong foreigners and was requested to appear before the authorities in London, along with many others from the South Coast, charged with piracy.

Of course, piracy did not start with the Hundred Years' War. The Norman Baron de Marisco established his own pirate fiefdom on Lundy Island in the Celtic Sea in the thirteenth century. He made the mistake of plotting to kill King Henry III, and was subsequently the first man to be hanged, drawn and quartered. This grotesque punishment, invented for de Marisco, was also used in Plymouth at a later date.

In April 1548 a commissioner trying to establish the English Prayer Book in the West Country was stabbed by a priest, and the priest's execution fuelled riots known as the 'Prayer Book Rebellion'. A protesting Cornish army gathered and headed east to attack Trematon Castle and then Plymouth, where they were met with guns on North Hill. It then proceeded further east to besiege Exeter, but the army was crushed. In fact, the King's troops

The beautifully elaborate title page of Cranmer's 1540 translation of the Bible: source of the Book of Common Prayer which sparked the Prayer Book Rebellion of 1548.

captured so many Cornishmen that they decided it would be most convenient to simply execute the prisoners on the spot. Nine hundred bound and gagged men were forced to their knees, and their throats slit one by one. It took just 10 minutes to murder all 900 of the prisoners. A Tesco store, Exeter Vale, now stands on the site of the massacre.

The gallows in Plymouth ended the lives of most of the remaining Cornish 'traitors', but one was chosen for the special treatment of being hanged, drawn and quartered. First, the doomed man was dragged by a horse from his cell along the cobbled streets up onto the Hoe. He was there hanged by the neck but cut down before he lost consciousness, then stretched out while his genitals were cut off, his stomach cut open and his intestines pulled slowly out from him. Finally, his heart was cut out and burned. He was forced to watch all of these actions. Of course, death followed very quickly after the last act, but the lifeless body was further desecrated – a horrific act in the days when people believed that the body should remain intact in readiness for the Rapture, when the dead would be resurrected and transported to heaven.

His head was cut off and set on a pole fixed to the Guildhall with 'cramps of iron', and his body cut into quarters. One quarter joined the head on a second pole, while another was carried by John Matthew to Tavistock. John Wylstrem was paid to perform the grisly execution and the under-sheriff of Cornwall was forced to watch, quite likely as a warning to his fellow Cornishmen never to attack Plymouth again.

Surprisingly the pirates from Plymouth never suffered the same fate, perhaps because they themselves were often men of high standing or protected by high-ranking benefactors. It was the high-ranking Hugh Courtenay from Cornwall who led a pirate attack on a Spanish ship moored in Plymouth in 1449. Though Hugh was a namesake of the illustrious Earl of Devon who had so successfully defended the town just fifty years earlier, he was no close relation, but he was still an important official. He escaped punishment and simply took his spoils back with him to Fowey.

As the aristocracy took the profits, the pirates themselves reduced in numbers, recruited into the wars against France and then Spain in the progression of the Tudor monarchs from King Henry VIII to Queen Elizabeth I.

However, as the coasts of the Americas were explored and exploited by the Spanish and Portuguese, the seas of the sixteenth century belonged to a new age of English pirates, raiding the same coasts and the Spanish settlements for gold and glory. But they were no longer pirates: with the backing of the crown, they were now officially privateers. For 100 years, more expeditions to the New World set out from Plymouth than from all the other English ports combined, and most were intent on theft.

Privateers and scourges of the Spanish: Sir Martin Frobisher, knighted for his services against the Armada, died in Plymouth on 15 November 1594. He once accidentally transported 1,550 tons of worthless iron pyrite from Canada to England, believing it to be gold. The other two men are Sir John Hawkins and Sir Francis Drake, whose adventures are described underneath.

'Hawkins the Slave Driver'

Sir John Hawkins was born in Plymouth in 1532 into an illustrious family of mayors, captains and merchants. While his older brother William was fitting the ships to defend Plymouth against the Spanish, John was hell-bent on a very different trade. From his early voyages to the Canary Islands, he learned that the Spanish were in need of slave labour, and in 1562 he set out for the Guinea coast to capture West Africans as slaves.

Hawkins was by no means the first slave-trader, but his genius was to systemise and legitimise the process. With important London backers, he set out with three ships and 100 men and raided Sierra Leone, taking or purchasing around 300 slaves. In the West Indies, he traded these prisoners for hides, ginger, pearls and sugar and returned to Plymouth wealthy and triumphant.

In 1564 he repeated the sickening 'Triangle'. Now backed by Queen Elizabeth I herself, his fleet travelled inland along the West African waterways and attacked the villages – and Hawkins' men were brutal in their efforts, eventually taking around 450 slaves to sell along the coasts of South America. At first the Spanish refused to trade the slaves: they had signed an exclusive trade agreement with the Portuguese, though they told Hawkins they might consider taking the slaves off his hands if he paid them 'import taxes'. Hawkins instead threatened to burn the town, whereupon the Spanish relented. Hawkins then returned to Plymouth in 1565 with a bounty of gold, silver, pearls and jewels, and a 60 per cent profit for his delighted investors. John Sparke, twice mayor of Plymouth, travelled with Hawkins and included the first mention of potatoes and tobacco in his diaries. Sir Walter Raleigh would be credited with their discovery, but it was Hawkins' men who saw them first.

Elizabeth I granted Sir John Hawkins with a coat of arms that included at the crest a bound African slave. Sir John was appointed 'Admiral to the Queen's Navy' – which in 1567 was residing in

Slaves exposed naked for sale at the end of the vile Triangle. (LC-USZ62-15395)

the Cattewater when fifty Spanish ships entered Plymouth Sound and failed to lower their flags in respect to the English fleet. Hawkins ordered his gunner to shoot the Spanish admiral's flag. The Spanish ignored his threat, and their flag remained flying – until Hawkins' next shot hit their ship. The Spanish flag was immediately lowered – but soon after, in the dead of night, a band of masked men boarded the Spanish ships and set free the Protestant Flemish seamen who the Spanish had captured to use as slaves; they had been chained to the oars in the galley. The Spanish Admiralty blamed Hawkins, failing to see the irony that Hawkins should be rescuing slaves. The incident would damage the prospects for Hawkins's future trading voyages.

In October 1567 Hawkins set off on his third slaving voyage, this time with five ships: the *Jesus of Lubeck*, the *Minion*, the *Angel*, the *William and John* and the *Judith*, the last commanded by his young cousin Francis Drake. Again they made their way to the Guinea coast, where they augmented their human cargo

by capturing the Portuguese slave ship *Madre de Deus* (Mother of God). Perhaps only a modern reader can appreciate the irony of the names of these god-forsaken vessels.

They headed to South America and while Hawkins was trading, Drake was sent ahead to Rio de la Hacha, where he was fired upon by Spanish forces, who were determined not to trade with these arrogant Englishmen. When Hawkins arrived, his men landed and took the town, selling eighty slaves there before deciding to head for home.

Hawkins' small fleet was then battered in a storm near Florida and they urgently made for the port of Vera Cruz to make repairs. In Vera Cruz, they were excited to discover Spanish treasure ships there awaiting the arrival of the Spanish fleet to escort them to Europe. However, they did not have the strength to seize them, so they peacefully tried to refit their ships. When the Spanish fleet reached the city, however, hostilities began – and suddenly the English ships found themselves under attack. All the Englishmen on shore were killed and the *Jesus* riddled with shot as Hawkins and his men jumped across to the *Minion*. Using the

City and port of Vera Cruz, where Hawkins' crew were tortured to death. (LC-USZ62-107854)

The Elizabethan House on New Street is a fine example of the Tudor houses built for sea captains. Narrow, but on three storeys – the spiral staircase winds around an old ship's mast – the house must have been very over-crowded when, in the 1800s, it was split into rooms to house a dozen families.

The ghost of an eight-year-old girl is thought to roam the first floor. She has been seen many times peering through the window onto the street, by those wandering past as well as visitors inside the house. Visitors and staff complain of ice-cold spots in the house. A cradle on the upper-most floor has been observed starting to rock all by itself, and heavy furniture has been heard scraping across the floor in the room above when no one else is in the building. Before I knew of the haunting, I myself visited the house, and felt one very cold spot on the first floor and an almost overwhelming urge to re-arrange the furniture...

The haunted Elizabethan House.

Jesus as a shield, the *Minion* and the *Judith* survived the attack, limping home – and leaving the survivors remaining in Vera Cruz to suffer imprisonment, torture and burning alive at the stake at the hands of the Spanish Inquisition.

Just over 100 years later, another Plymouth sailor was captured by the Inquisition at Vera Cruz: he swiftly converted to Catholicism and saved his life. A Frenchman called Louis Ramé recorded his treatment at the hands of the Inquisition at this time after he refused to convert: he was clapped in irons and kept in a dark cell for years on end, fed on drugged food that eventually drove him close to madness.

The treachery of the Spanish fleet hardened Drake and Hawkins against the Spanish and Catholicism. Drake's family had earlier been left homeless by a Catholic Rebellion and the embittered, half-starved men arriving back in Devon were determined to avenge themselves against the Spanish Catholics. Hawkins' revenge was subtle. In 1571 he became a spy, pretending to be part of a plot to betray Queen Elizabeth I, while offering his services to the Spanish in return for releasing some English prisoners of war. Sir John's ruse succeeded and, gaining the trust of the Spanish, he discovered and foiled the Spaniards' plans to invade England. But in 1588, the Spanish would return in greater numbers than ever before.

To protect England, Drake was said to have sold his soul to Satan at Devil's Point, a headland in Plymouth Sound near Devonport, notorious for its dangerous currents. In 1588 it was rumoured that Drake met at Devil's Point with a coven of witches and concocted the terrible storms that drove the Spanish Armada north and west, away from England's shores. If you are on Devil's Point in July, in the early morning fog, it is said that you will hear the disembodied voices of Drake and his coven raising the winds that blew the Spanish away. While at Devil's Point, Drake whittled on a stick: each wood shaving that fell into the Sound, it was claimed, formed a mighty fire-ship that brought death and destruction to the Armada. If Drake really did do a deal with Satan, it is good to know that, in July 1588, Satan was on the side of the English.

Drake and the Devil

Sir Francis Drake's heroic image stands proud on Plymouth Hoe and in Tavistock, the town of his birth – but over the centuries the stories of his daring exploits have all been linked with witchcraft and devil-worship.

Francis was the eldest of twelve sons living with his family in Tavistock when their farm was attacked in the midst of the 1549 Western Rebellion. The family fled to Plymouth. The young Francis was apprenticed to the sea and ended up working for his cousin, John Hawkins. After the horror of Vera Cruz, Francis Drake took his own revenge on the Spanish by theft – no longer was he a trader, but a patriotic pirate. Sheltering in a small natural harbour he called Port Pheasant, he surveyed the Spanish treasure port of Nombre de Dios, a small shanty town that twice a year loaded up the treasure ships with gold and silver mined in Peru and Bolivia. Drake's plan was to fortify Port Pheasant and from there to raid the treasure ships.

In 1572 Drake returned to Port Pheasant with two ships, the *Pasco* and the *Swan*, with his brothers John and Joseph, and enlarged his forces by enlisting the local Cimarrons – by dreadful irony, a group of escaped slaves who hated the Spanish. In July, Drake's forces made their first attack on Nombre de Dios, sixty men stealing into the town and heading for the battery of guns on the shore. Drake led forty of his men into the town, beating drums and sounding trumpets. The inhabitants, thinking they were being attacked by a sizeable force, fled in terror, but a small force of musketeers bravely remained behind and took on Drake's men in the market square. Drake's trumpeter was killed and Drake was shot in the leg.

A second force, led by Drake's brother John, then attacked the Spaniards from behind, and the two brothers headed for the governor's house where the gold and silver were stored. Just as the Spanish forces were re-grouping, a thunderstorm struck and soaked Drake's men and their weapons, leaving them dispirited and defenceless (their gunpowder being sodden). Drake urged on his men, only to discover that the governor's stores were empty – too late! The treasure ships had left just weeks before.

Drake managed to escape, bleeding but alive. He then decided to wait for the next delivery of gold and silver, coming via mule train from Panama to Venta Cruces, but his brothers did not survive the wait. John died from wounds he suffered during the failed raid on Nombre de Dios, and Joseph – like many of Drake's men – succumbed to yellow fever. The raids on the Spanish mule trains from Panama failed too, and with his ships now unfit for the journey home, Drake's voyage was turning into a disaster.

A chance meeting with a French privateer called Guillaume le Testu changed their fortunes. Le Testu told Drake of another mule train laden with treasure heading for Nombre de Dios and their combined forces successfully captured 190 mules, each carrying 300 pounds of silver. Le Testu lost his life, but Drake managed to steal a Spanish galleon and returned home at last in 1573 with £100,000 worth of gold and 15 tons of silver ingots.

Drake accused Thomas Doughty of witchcraft, mutiny and treason on extremely tenuous grounds – the arrival of a sudden storm. Doughty was beheaded. (LC-USZ62-135589)

In 1577 Drake set out with a small fleet, telling everyone he was heading for Alexandria, when in fact he was determined to try his hand at sailing around the Strait of Magellan and into the Pacific Ocean, for the first time, to investigate any Spanish settlements worth raiding along the western coast of South America.

The first few weeks of the voyage were a catastrophe. By the time his fleet had reached South America's eastern coastline, they had already lost one boy overboard and been attacked by Moroccan pirates; an attempted mutiny then resulted in the execution of his former friend Thomas Doughty on the shores of Port Julian. In the end, only the *Golden Hind* made it into the Pacific.

As he was setting out to sea, Drake's first wife, Mary Newman, agreed to wait for him for seven years before considering marrying again. Before the seven years were up, however, thinking she would never see him again, she agreed to marry one of her many suitors. As they stood at the altar about to become husband and wife, a cannon ball crashed down between them. It is said that Drake fired the shot from the Antipodes as a warning, to remind his wife of her promise.

Drake soon found himself under attack from the Spanish and unable to travel north or south, so, in a desperate effort to return home, he steered the *Golden Hind* westward and faced a brutal journey across the Pacific, finally returning to Plymouth in 1580, laden with treasure and stories of adventures in the Spice Islands, as the first Englishman to circumnavigate the globe.

Drake's finest hour, however, came with the defeat of the Spanish Armada. In 1587 Queen Elizabeth I was suspicious that the King of Spain was intending to invade England and she sent Drake to engage the Spanish fleet in a pre-emptive strike. Taking four of her largest battleships, Drake burned King Philip's fleet while they were still moored in Cadiz Harbour. On his way home, Drake managed to take the Spanish merchant ship *San Filipe* – which had £1 million in treasure on board.

In revenge, King Philip of Spain created the most powerful armada of ships Europe had ever seen, and – mustering 55,000 men for the fight – prepared to invade England. However, luck was not with the Spanish. Its first commander, the Marquis of Santa Cruz, died in February 1588, and was replaced by Medina-Sidonia who, though high-ranking, had no experience of the sea. Their army was reduced by disease to 16,000 and many of the men were ill-equipped. The fleet was then delayed by bad weather, with five of its major ships forced to leave the fleet before they'd even sighted the English coast.

The English fleet mustered in defence, a rag-tag mix of Navy ships and privateers, was greater in number – 200 ships to 130 of the Spanish – but the Spanish firepower was twice that of the English. The key to the success of the English fleet came from Hawkins' brilliance as a shipwright, designing smaller 'race-built' ships, highly manoeuvrable in the midst of battle. The English fleet waited in Plymouth Sound for news of the Spaniards' approach.

On 19 July 1588 Drake and his captains were playing bowls on the Hoe when Captain Thomas Fleming, a fellow privateer, brought his merchant ship into the Sound and rushed over to the party to announce he had sighted the Spanish Armada approaching. Drake is famous for calmly declaring before the breathless Fleming that they still had time to finish their game – but of course they could not make sail if the wind and tides were against them.

When the English finally engaged with the Spanish, it was at daybreak on 21 July 1588, just off the Eddystone Rocks, a treacherous reef 10 miles south of the Rame peninsula. The English had the wind in their favour, and their small ships quickly avoided the Spanish attacks. Drake

If the sightings are true, Sir Francis Drake still haunts Boringdon Hall, originally one of the Saxon manors in Plympton that changed hands when the Normans invaded. It was a popular residence for the Elizabethan heroes, and Queen Elizabeth I herself once stayed there while visiting the West Country. Sir Francis appears in the Great Hall at Boringdon, in his full armour, his sword at the ready.

The Ship Inn in Exeter famously barred Sir Francis Drake because of his drunken behaviour, but this hasn't stopped him coming back to haunt the current owners…

captured much-needed gunpowder from the Spanish ships, but his tactics left the English fleet in disarray, and it took a day for them to regroup and catch up to the Spanish, who were by then making their way along the English coast to Portland.

An attack at the Isle of Wight sent the Armada fleeing to Calais, where the English attacked again, with eight fire-ships, warships filled with pitch, brimstone, gunpowder and tar and set alight, cast downwind in the direction of the Armada. Medinia-Sidonia's flagship held its ground, bravely facing these floating fire-bombs, but the rest of the fleet scattered in confusion.

Sidonia then regrouped his fleet near Gravelines in the Spanish Netherlands, but Drake had learned a few of their tactics, realising that the gunners were instructed to fire just once and then head for the rigging to make ready for boarding the enemy ships. The quick English ships provoked the Spanish into firing but managed to stay out of range, and concentrated their own fire on damaging the Spanish ships below the water-line. After eight hours of continuous fighting, the English, running out of ammunition, were forced to use anything at hand to load the cannons. By late afternoon, the English were forced to pull back. But the damage to the Spanish ships was extensive, with two galleons run aground and the Spanish exhausted: the battle was finally over.

The threat of invasion was still present, however, and on 8 August 1588 Queen Elizabeth I gave probably her most famous speech in Tilbury, amidst a force making ready to defend London:

I know I have the body of a weak and feeble woman; but I have the heart and stomach of a king – and of a King of England too, and think foul scorn that Parma or Spain, or any prince of Europe, should dare to invade the borders of my realm, to which, rather than any dishonour should grow by me, I myself will take up arms – I myself will be your general, judge and rewarder of every one of your virtues in the field…

Of all the privateers, Drake was Elizabeth's favourite. He brought her wealth, success and popularity few Kings or Queens of England would ever attain.

Above *The English grapple with the Spanish Armada, firing anything to hand.*

Left *Elizabeth I as a young woman.*

A COFFIN AND TWO JUDGES

JUDGE JOHN GLANVILLE (1542-1600) – whose effigy at Tavistock lost part of its nose during the Civil War – was famous in Plymouth for ruthless judgements administered without favour or bias – even going so far as to have his own daughter executed for murder, or so the story goes.

His daughter, Elizabeth Glanville, fell in love with a Naval Lieutenant called George Stanwich, but her father disapproved and forced her to marry a Plymouth goldsmith called Sir John Page – sometimes known as 'old Page' or 'wealthy Page' – who was considered by many to be a miser. Page lived in a house on Woolster Street which subsequently became Mayoralty House, and here the miser met his death. (The house no longer exists, subsumed under the extension of the Guildhall when it was rebuilt after the bombings of the Second World War.) It seems that Elizabeth, with the help of her maid and her lover, murdered her bridegroom-to-be, either shortly before or after the marriage. A neighbour reported overhearing a man in the street softly calling up to the Page house: 'For God's sake, hold your hand!'

A female voice replied from within: ''Tis too late: the deed is done.'

The next morning, Elizabeth tried to claim that her husband had perished

---

ANOTHER MURDER!: In 1874 one Sylvanus Sweet smashed in his wife's head with a cutlass. As she lay dying, he got a cab to the police station and gave himself up, admitting he'd murdered her because she was trying to have him sent to a lunatic asylum. It emerged that he suffered frequently from epileptic fits and there was a history of madness in the family. His wife had left him a year before as they discussed divorce proceedings, but she had recently returned to give him one last chance. It was indeed to be one last chance. And Sweet was found guilty but insane.

suddenly of natural causes during the night, but the neighbour spoke out and the body was exhumed: clear signs of strangulation were revealed. Elizabeth and her accomplices were subsequently brought before Judge Glanville for sentencing. He had them all hanged. The murder of 'wealthy Page' and the trial of Glanville's daughter were later transformed into a play called *The Lamentable Tragedy of Page of Plymouth,* in which Glanville's daughter re-enacts the vicious killing of her husband.

However, even at the time the story of the father Glanville executing his own daughter was considered to be untrue. It was possibly confused with the more reliable story of Judge Hody, who sat in judgement on the public assizes during the reigns of Henrys VII and VIII. Hody was presented with his own son, Thomas, who had confessed to a capital crime. He was forced to pronounce a sentence of death upon the boy. Thomas killed himself in prison before the executioner could take him, whereupon the father denounced his son as a degenerate. He refused to attend the boy's funeral – and since that day, it is said, no boy has been christened Thomas in the Hody family.

Returning to the Glanvilles and the 'wealthy Page': in St Andrew's church, near the Guildhall, the church officials were breaking the ground near the communion table to inter the body of a lady called Lovell, when, to their surprise, they discovered another coffin already buried there, with the inscription of 'wealthy Page'.

When opened, Page's remains were found to be in a surprisingly perfect state, but crumpled to dust on being exposed to the air. The coffin and its contents drew hundreds of curious Plymouth citizens over the next few days, with many relics stolen as souvenirs, including the nails from the coffin. So if the 'wealthy Page' existed, perhaps the story of Judge Glanville could be true.

There is another version of the story, however, telling of a relative of Judge Granville, a Tavistock merchant by the name of Glandfeeld. Glandfeeld's daughter Eulalia fell in love with her father's lowly assistant Strangwich, but Glandfeeld forced his daughter to marry the wealthy Page instead. After the marriage, Strangwich visited Eulalia as her lover, and they plotted to kill her husband, bribing two servants to do the deed. The servants found Page in his bedchamber, stifled his mouth with a handkerchief and, throwing him onto the bed, broke Page's neck. When apprehended, Eulalia confessed all to the mayor and Sir Francis Drake – and if a story is to be embellished, who better to include? The lovers were then hanged at Barnstaple, as Exeter was suffering another outbreak of plague.

But if Judge Glanville's daughter was not the culprit hanged by her own father, then why does Glanville, tormented, apparently still haunt his Devon family estate, Kilworthy House? And why does his daughter also haunt the estate, appearing as an ominous spectre, missing her head?

TO BE A PILGRIM

THE PILGRIMS OF the *Mayflower* were not the first English settlers in the New World, but they were among the first to survive the ordeal. In 1579 Sir Humphrey Gilbert claimed the first English base in Newfoundland, comprising mainly Portuguese and French fishing villages, but he sank with his ship in a storm before making it home.

Sir Walter Raleigh, one of Plymouth's favourite courtiers, then took possession of North Carolina in the name of Queen Elizabeth I, but the first settlement there left 108 emigrants starving. They were then massacred by Native Americans. A second settlement simply disappeared: only the bones of a single man were ever found.

The third wave of settlers, led by John White, again disappeared. John briefly visited Plymouth to get supplies and returned to the American settlement to find everyone in his colony had vanished – including his wife and their daughter. Search parties found no trace, but there is a story that pale, red-haired children were born to a native tribe not far north of John White's settlement... These small groups were easy prey to the natives.

In 1605 Captain Weymouth arrived in Plymouth, having explored the St George's River and Penobscot in the New World and returning with five Native Americans on board (taken by force during failed negotiations with their tribes). Tisquantum, Manida and Shetwarroes were handed over as a prize to the commander of the Hoe Fort, Sir Ferdinando Gorges, who taught them English and forced them to stay with him for three years. Two of the natives, Manida and Shetwarroes, then helped the Plymouth Company establish a settlement in Maine, but the capture, kidnap and treatment of these first allies did little to secure the natives' trust. Cold, disease and famine eventually brought yet another failed colony limping back to Plymouth.

Captain John Smith, an adventurer, created a more positive impression with the natives, though not until he was saved by Pocahontas, the big-hearted daughter of the great chief Powhatan. Smith was dragged before Chief Powhatan and his

Above *Pocahontas saving Captain Smith.*
(LC-DIG-pga-02687)

Left *Portrait drawn during 'Mrs Rolfe's' visit to England in 1616. (LC-USZ62-8104)*

head placed on a rock, ready for the tribe to beat his brains out. Suddenly, Powhatan's daughter Pocahontas, just twelve years old, laid her own head on Smith's – kill him and you kill your favourite daughter too, she told him. Powhatan conceded and let the Englishman live.

Pocahontas was subsequently captured by the English, as part of hostage negotiations, and she eventually married John Rolfe, a tobacco farmer. She became a Christian and changed her name to Rebecca. In June 1616 Pocahontas (or Rebecca Rolfe, as she was now known) arrived in Plymouth with sixteen of her

Powhatan tribe, including Tomocomo, a shaman, who tried to keep a tally of the English he saw by marking notches on a stick, but soon grew tired of it – these English were just too many to count. Probably this was the first time the Native Americans realised that these English settlers were to become a serious threat through sheer weight of numbers.

As she was about to return to her native land, Pocahontas died of a mysterious illness, leaving her infant son in the care of Sir Lewis Stucley (remembered by history as the man who betrayed Sir Walter Raleigh to his death at the hands of King James I's executioner). Pocahontas' shaman friend Tomocomo returned to his homeland unimpressed by the English and his brief meeting with King James I, who had not even offered him a present.

With King James on the throne, Plymouth's fortunes worsened. Elizabeth had been no friend to religious non-conformists in the town, but her Plymouth 'pirates' were her fortune and she was always ready to turn a blind eye where money was concerned; her favourite, Drake, was of Puritan stock, after all. James I instead decided to make peace with Catholic Spain and enforced religious conformity throughout England, and a small group of Puritans, with links to Plymouth's Puritan merchants, found themselves forced to flee to Holland to avoid King James' militia. In time even Holland became unsafe, and the desperate group of pilgrims applied for a grant of land in Virginia where they might live and worship freely.

The pilgrims chartered two ships, the *Mayflower* and the *Speedwell*, but the latter failed to live up to its name. By the time they berthed in Plymouth to repair the leaking *Speedwell*, it was agreed that the voyage would be made only on the *Mayflower*, carrying just 102 men, women and children, a quarter of the original number.

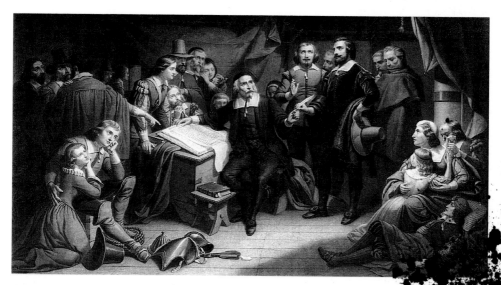

Pilgrims aboard the Mayflower *– little did they realise what horrors awaited them on the coast of the New World. (LC-USZ61-206)*

Above *A rather fanciful portrayal of the landing on Plymouth Rock, engraved by Joseph Andrews in 1869. (LC-USZ62-4060)*

Left *A view of the Barbican, with the memorial archway leading to the Mayflower Steps in the distance. These are not the original steps, as the quays at the Barbican have changed dramatically over the centuries.*

Half of these weren't even Puritans but 'strangers' replacing Puritan settlers who had decided against the voyage at the last minute. It is impossible now to imagine how they could contemplate taking three pregnant women and twenty-three children on such a perilous venture. Their allies in Plymouth were hospitable, and prayers for a successful voyage were offered. They were not answered: the *Mayflower* set off across the Atlantic on 6 September 1620, and into a nightmare.

For sixty-five days, the *Mayflower* fought her way across the Atlantic in terrifying storms, and the nauseated passengers crowded into a warren of small rooms between the leaky decks, barely 5ft high. Their late departure left them travelling in November, rather than the balmy summer planned. They were out of firewood, two of the settlers were already dead and scurvy was setting in.

The pilgrims were weavers, tailors and shoemakers, not adventurers with the skills required to carve out a settlement in the wilderness. Their success was founded on stoic resolve to create not just a settlement but a new way of living, under the leadership of John Carver, a man of humility, who would successfully bring together the disparate factions on board to work to a common cause.

With inadequate maps amidst stormy conditions, the navigator was sailing 'blind', and they arrived not at their destination but many miles north, at Cape Cod. An attempt to sail south nearly brought destruction in the Pollack Rip, a treacherous maze of shoals and sandbars. Surviving only by a fortunate change in the wind, they limped back to Cape Cod. Though beautiful, it was a sandy harbour, a wilderness inadequate for a plantation, and they were 500 miles from the nearest English settlement. And it was starting to snow. New England snow.

They had to steal from the natives' stores of corn to stay alive. The nearest tribes had good reason to hate the English on their 'floating islands': a previous ship had captured many of their men and shot them in cold blood. The pilgrims' first attempt to explore and find a decent location for their settlement put them at the mercy of a rain of arrows as the natives opened fire.

On 20 December 1620 the pilgrims finally decided upon a permanent settlement near Plymouth Rock. The land had much to commend it – a 165ft hill gave them defence and a good view, and there was an unusually good supply of fresh water. What they couldn't see was the area's infected history. Three years before the pilgrims landed, the area had been populated by around 1,500 natives, the shores dotted with hundreds of wigwams and fields of corn. But 1619, just before the arrival of the pilgrims, an epidemic hit the land, one which left only skulls and bones dotted around Plymouth Rock. The pilgrims had unfortunately chosen a site of pestilence, and during the next four months half of the pilgrims would perish.

But still the survivors were determined to flourish. One indentured servant on the voyage, John Howland, managed to survive falling off the *Mayflower* in the middle of the Atlantic. He'd gone on deck, desperate for some air, and the gales tossed him overboard. Even though he was pulled 10ft under the stormy waters, John wouldn't let go of a trailing rope and they managed to bring him back on board. He went on to have ten children and an astonishing eighty-eight grandchildren, all of the same hardy constitution as their grandfather.

AD 1608

TO BE A PIRATE

KING JAMES I made peace with Spain, and forced many seafarers into unemployment. No longer were the West Indies the source of stolen Spanish treasure; no more would privateers have a royal licence to steal gold and silver from the Americas. In 1608 four pirates were executed and buried at Plymouth, arrested by Sir Richard Hawkins, Vice Admiral of Devon and son of the celebrated Sir John Hawkins. When Sir Walter Raleigh stole Spanish gold in Guiana, he was declared a traitor to the new King and beheaded. Plymothians were unimpressed by the King's treatment of their favourite courtier.

So the pirates moved their criminal dealings to new shores in North Africa, and built ocean-going vessels for their new allies, the 'Turkish corsairs' – many built by a Plymouth-born man called William Bishop. But these developments brought new dangers back to English waters. In 1625 Sir James Bagge, the corrupt official in charge of Plymouth Sound, reported that a Turkish pirate ship had attacked three Cornish fishing boats and a ship from Dartmouth. The crews were either killed or taken as slaves to work the Turkish ships – which ironically had been designed by William Bishop!

Suddenly foreign slavers were raiding the coasts of Devon and Cornwall, stealing away fleets of fishermen to take as slaves, or women from the villages to sell in the markets in North Africa and the Middle East. The Mayor of Plymouth complained to the King that 1,000 Plymothians had been captured – though this was probably a slight exaggeration, it still reveals the fear of piracy that haunted the shores, keeping fishing fleets from going out and putting impossible pressures on the customs officers and local Navy forces to defend the coast.

Corsairs dogged the merchant ships making for Plymouth. One Moroccan ship passing Plymouth Sound was taken, and actually brought into the Cattewater as a prize. The courts railed against it all, but it seems they could not trust their own Navy or the local Plymouth authorities to prevent it. Corrupt local officials were often sequestering foreign ships and pillaging the contents for themselves. The pirate chief of Devon, Captain Nutt, paid his men so well that the sailors of the Royal Navy frequently 'jumped ship', and the Plymouth merchants were forced to pay for their own protection. Plymouth's maritime status and reputation deteriorated rapidly.

Sir John Eliot, Vice Admiral of Devon, tried to put paid to all the corruption, He regularly hanged captured corsairs and tried to get Captain Nutt put into gaol. However, it seems that Nutt had powerful friends in high places and it was Sir John Eliot who, conspired against, eventually found himself in gaol – held on a charge, ironically, of corruption, accused of accepting a £500 bribe from Nutt to release him.

The Reluctant Pirate

Not all pirates, however, were cruel cut-throats. Born in Plymouth of lowly status, Captain White was in the merchant service in Barbados when he was captured by a French pirate who took him and his crew as slaves, and burnt and sank his brig-antine. The crew were then used as target practice by the pirates.

Captain White and what remained of his crew eventually escaped the pirates and paddled in a long boat to Augustin Bay. There they found themselves strangers in a strange land, with no transport to make their way home, so they agreed to join another pirate ship captained by William Read. Read steered a course for Madagascar and White reluctantly assisted in Read's raid on the Bay of St Augustine.

The raid was a disaster, but White survived, and after many adventures – and forced service aboard many a pirate ship on his quest to reach home – he found himself captain of his own pirate ship, where he was noted for gallantry and a generous nature.

He eventually retired, with an enormous fortune, at Hopeful Point, Madagascar, built a house, raised cattle, and found himself a woman by whom he had a son. But the lure of pirate adventures was too much, and White decided to join a Captain Halsey on just one more raiding party. It would be his last. He would never make it back to England. He returned after the raids very ill, and died six months later. His last wish was that his son be taken to England aboard the first ship that passed. Some years later, this wish was fulfilled when an English ship touched in at the harbour and the boys' guardians faithfully discharged Smith's last wishes – the boy was adopted by the English captain and brought up to become a good man and to live a better life than his father.

Blood Lust and Henry Avery

Henry Avery, or Every, was also born in Plymouth. The son of an innkeeper, like White he joined the Royal Navy heading out to the West Indies, but there end any similarities. Avery soon grew tired of the naval life and mutinied, setting the captain off in a boat and taking the ship for himself.

Re-naming the ship the *Fancy* (a little bit of what you fancy...?), Avery and his crew set out to be pirates in the Red Sea, preying on the wealthy merchant ships sailing between India and the Middle East. The sixth ship he captured, the *Fateh Mahomed*, was carrying gold and silver worth £50,000. His next was to be the most famous pirate prize ever taken: the *Gang-i-Sawai*, 'the Exceeding Treasure'.

The *Gang-i-Sawai* was owned by the Great Mogul and carried a large crew and sixty-two guns: too much of a match for Avery's ship on its own, but helpless

Treasure coming aboard Henry Avery's ship, the Fancy. (Avery is the man on the left.)

against the fleet Avery assembled to take her. Avery's first shot managed to damage the *Gang-i-Sawai's* main mast, and one of her Indian cannons blew up on deck. While the fighting continued, Avery's allies secretly circled the ship and boarded her. The desperate defenders suddenly found themselves surrounded by Avery's men, just as the *Fancy* came up alongside.

What happened next on the *Gang-i-Sawai* is nothing short of a horror story. The pirates had made one of the largest hauls in history, each man receiving £1,000, but the money was not enough for these blood-thirsty men. The crew of the *Gang-i-Sawai* were tortured until they revealed the location of any further treasures hidden on board, and then slaughtered. In the course of these horrors, the pirates discovered that several women were on board, disguised as men to shield them from the pirates' attentions. An elderly relative of the Mogul, along with her servants and all of the female passengers, were savagely assaulted for several days. A number of the victims died. One passenger killed himself, his wife and their servant to avoid being made to watch the carnage and depravity, while others threw themselves overboard in despair.

Days later, the *Fancy* and the other two pirate ships finally left, and the discovery of the *Gang-i-Sawai* and its tortured passengers caused an international outcry. The English were forced to make a very humbling apology to the Great Mogul to ensure trading relations, and promised to catch and execute every one of Avery's men.

Avery, in the meantime, suggested to his fellow pirate captains that all of the loot would be best held aboard the *Fancy* until they reached a safe harbour at Madagascar. This was agreed – the other captains not being very bright – and the following morning they awoke to discover Avery had sailed off with all the spoils. In the Bahamas, a bribe to the Governor assured Avery's safety and he quietly disappeared.

After an expensive international man-hunt, the English managed to find only six of Avery's loathsome crew, who were duly hanged. Avery himself escaped justice and disappeared into wealthy obscurity.

AD 1675

THE BURNING GIRL

SUMMER 1675, AND the day began like any other for the Weeks family in Plymouth. Mr Weeks prepared to go to work; he ran a business dyeing cloth. His widowed daughter, Mary Pengelly, lived with him and was busy feeding her own infant daughter – with the help of Philippa Carey, a nurse in her twenties whom Mr Weeks had employed to help with the baby. Fifteen-year-old Anne Evans served Mrs Elizabeth Weeks her porridge. Anne was their indentured servant, an orphan 'bound' to the Weeks family three years before by the Plymouth Corporation, following the death of her mother. It was a normal day.

But, as in all families, there were tensions. Anne was unhappy with her lot, and had been overheard declaring that she wanted to run away. Mrs Weeks was a tough employer who, a few days earlier, had argued with Philippa Carey, accusing the nurse of adultery. Carey, apparently estranged from her husband, had openly admitted her sin and declared that it was none of Mrs Weeks' business.

So, on this particular summer's day, Mrs Weeks demanded her porridge and

Anne Evans served it. Philippa Carey poured a mug of beer for Mr Weeks – beer was a more healthy option than water in the seventeenth century – but Mr Weeks declared the beer tasted 'odd' and passed the mug to his daughter Mary, who agreed – it did taste odd.

Suddenly Mrs Weeks did not feel well. She vomited, and went into severe convulsions. She was put to bed in agony, but died just a few hours later. As Mrs Weeks lay dying, Mr Weeks and Mary also fell ill, stricken by terrible stomach pains. Mr Weeks recovered, but his daughter worsened and soon followed her mother to the grave.

Faced with this sudden and inexplicable disaster, Mr Weeks could see only one solution: 'poison!' he cried, pointing an accusing finger at the servants. Anne was brought before the mayor for questioning and declared that she had bought a pot of groats (a mix of whole grain cereals) in the market. However, when they were made into porridge she claimed to have found a yellow substance in the pot. The family must have eaten this, she said, and been

Poor Anne Evans was burnt at the stake in Plymouth. (LC-USZ62-5922)

the beer into the porridge – the same beer that Philippa poured for Mr Weeks. The more Anne talked, the more elaborate her story became.

The questioning continued for weeks, the girls forced to remain in the sordid accommodation of Plymouth gaol, next to the Guildhall. Philippa Evans steadfastly denied any involvement in the murders, but Anne's story became increasingly wild.

At last the two girls appeared before the Lent Assizes in Exeter. The jury proclaimed them guilty of the murder of Elizabeth Weeks and Mary Pengelly, and the judge refused the girls' plea for transportation. Philippa Carey was sentenced to be hanged, while poor Anne Evans was to be burned at the stake. Anne's sentence was rare in Britain. Burning at the stake was more common in Europe, particularly for heretics or witches, but Anne Evans was neither a heretic nor a witch, but something worse, perhaps – a servant who had murdered her mistress. And for that, she had to be made an example of.

The sentence would normally have been carried out in Exeter, but the grieving Mr Weeks, a justice of the peace, was adamant that the girls should be seen to be punished for their crimes in Plymouth. It was agreed that the girls would be taken to Plymouth and executed on the Thursday before Easter, just two weeks later.

Philippa Carey tried to stay the execution by declaring she was pregnant, but the midwives could find no proof of this. The supposed father of the child was not revealed. Carey was later described as a widow, so her husband may have died while she was suffering in Plymouth gaol. He may even have been the murderer: when Philippa was asked to confess her

accidentally poisoned. In her testimony, Anne mentioned the argument between Mrs Weeks and Philippa Carey; Carey in her turn confirmed this, before accusing Anne Evans of the murders. The mayor realised there was no love lost between the servants, and played one girl against the other – and the servants damned each other to death.

On hearing Carey's accusations, Anne changed her story. She had, she said, found a packet of rat's poison in the house and Philippa had encouraged her to put some in Mrs Weeks' porridge to teach the old lady a lesson. Anne had then seen Philippa brewing the crushed poison into a beer and had told Anne to put some of

crime, she replied 'it may be that vile person, my husband, had a hand in it, but he is gone'.

One man who kept a close eye on the proceedings of the trial was John Quick, a non-conformist minister who himself had been repeatedly gaoled for preaching against the established Church. Just after the trial he wrote a book, *Hell Open'd, or the Infernal Sin of Murther Punished, Being a True Relation of the Poysoning of a Whole Family in Plymouth, Whereof Two Died in a Short Time*. He was a devout man, firmly believing in the redemptive powers of confession and adamant that the two girls confess their crimes, for 'it was as easie going to heaven from the stake and gallows as from their beds; and when their souls were departing from their bodies, God's holy angels would convey them into Paradise'. But Philippa Carey remained defiant, insisting on her innocence.

As the prisoners were brought from Exeter on horseback, thousands joined the procession at Plymouth. Quick tells us that the nurse exchanged ribald and obscene jests with the spectators.

Quick was gravely concerned for the morality of Plymouth. In the 1670s, Plymouth seemed populated with wicked sinners, undeterred by severe punishments. Malefactors were hanged in chains in public view, or branded and hanged, and the prisons were over-crowded with men and women locked in together in stinking cells.

In 1676 one John Codmore was hanged for admitting twenty-eight offences including horse stealing and the sale of his wife to a miller for £5. He was one of many hangings. As the ministers prayed, the condemned convicts either wept and pleaded for a quick death on the gallows, or angrily cursed the ministers and the spectators as they sang Psalms to strike the devil from the town. Executions were a public display of exorcism. Everywhere he looked, Quick saw sin and debauchery, and he was determined to turn this Sodom of Plymouth into a new Jerusalem –

The ducking stool was awarded to Plymouth as part of its incorporation as a town, and was in regular use in the punishment of women. The equipment was set on the edge of Sutton Pool and guilty women would be strapped and girdled into the seat – the 'cage' – and then lowered by rope into the filthy, freezing water below. In 1598 Mrs Cook and Mrs Coyt were both ducked for being scolds, and in 1607 Joseph Gubbs was paid to duck another wicked wife. Illegally selling wares directly to the ships was enough to get a woman ducked in 1657 – she would be fined, strapped into the stool and then hauled up three times.

A typical ducking stool of the era, showing the loop which was used to lower the chair into the water.

starting with the souls of Anne Evans and Philippa Carey.

The execution was anticipated as a rare spectacle, for there had not been a burning at Plymouth before. While the girls remained in Plymouth gaol, their gaolers were selling tickets to the leering crowd. Quick advised Anne Evans not to fear the fire: she had confessed, and therefore God would carry her through the ordeal; the flames, he said, would hurt her body but not her soul. In contrast, he advised the defiant Carey that she had made a terrible deal with the Devil and would go to hell. Angry with Carey's refusal to confess, he described her in the most memorable of terms: '[her] brow is of brass, she is impudent and hath a whore's forehead. If there were a very daughter of Hell, this was one in her proper colours.'

As he counselled and admonished the prisoners, a gallows and a stake were being erected on Prince Rock, the highest point of Plymouth, near the Cattewater.

On the appointed day, all of Plymouth was on or around Prince Rock: at least 10,000 people were waiting, eager for the spectacle. The mayor, the under-sheriff and the executioner were barely able to make it through the crowd. Anne Evans was carried on a wicker sledge from Plymouth gaol to the stake. She lay curled up on her left side, her Bible under her arm, shocked into immobility as though she was already dead. She was then pinned to the stake by an iron hoop, while Carey was positioned downwind, standing on a ladder beneath the hanging rope. Quick said prayers and the crowd and poor Evans joined in, singing a Psalm. Evans was offered strong drink to support her 'in her last agonies with Death and conflicts with the Devil'.

A rope was wrapped around Anne Evans' neck, but the executioner was all for setting the wood alight beneath her before she was strangled. The crowd, in pity, demanded that the rope be tightened first, and the block taken from beneath her feet, and soon she fell, strangled to death. It took a further fifteen minutes before the executioner could get the wood to light and the first smoke blew into the face of Philippa Carey, forced to watch

---

By today's standards, the punishments in early Plymouth seem unduly harsh. In the fifteenth century, a thief would be hanged. Women thought to be whores or of ill-repute were whipped, many then exiled from the town. In 1590, Thomas Payne was paid to whip six whores. A woman's fidelity was paramount, and in the 1540s Joanne Collins brought a suit against John Meyow for apparently forcing her to have sexual relations with him on promise of marriage and then reneging on his promise, leaving her unmarried, with child and in disgrace. Joanne's fidelity was her main defence: 'she being an honest maid and replete with the many honest and womanly qualities as well as the gifts of nature as of grace and fortune'.

She then added that he 'provoked her to consent unto his filthy lust of the flesh... abusing her body so that he hath begotten her with child' by force of arms, threatening her with a dagger. To avoid a whipping, Joanne had to prove she had been raped at knifepoint.

There are very few reports of witchcraft in Plymouth, though Bracken (1931) and Whitfield (1900) were adamant that it was being secretly practised in Plymouth.

Scores of women and men were hanged in Devon in the last half of the seventeenth century, suspected of practising the dark arts. Fear of witches gave the constables the authority to drive any unsavoury characters out of the town, usually accompanied by a beating. In 1801, Peter and Grace Steel were accused of being fortune tellers and committed to the 'house of correction'. In 1804, Deborah Tanner suspected her neighbour, Ann Raddon, of being a witch – and stuck a pin in her to test her theory. Ann Raddon complained about this, and Deborah was forced by the court to apologise. Plymouth refused to countenance witchcraft in any form – but in the meantime, those wishing to consult with a practising witch just had to cross the Tamar into Cornwall.

Early engraving of a witch, pictured riding backwards upon a goat. Magical powers could often be detected – well, according to Witch-Finder General Matthew Hopkins, anyway – by a spot upon the body that was impervious to pain. Deborah Tanner was trying to detect this spot when she thrust a pin into Ann Raddon. (LC-USZ62-123495)

the burning for two hours before she too was executed.

When it came to hanging Carey, however, the executioner could not be found. A search discovered him hiding, drunk and senseless – overwhelmed by the horror of the occasion. A second executioner was appointed and at last Carey was hanged. Carey's last words were solemn: 'Judge and revenge my cause, O God,' she said. This Quick took as proof that she 'went into a lake of brimstone and fire, there to be tormented for ever and ever.' Actually, it was very likely she was innocent.

AD 1660-1822

DEAD MAN'S LOTTERY – A SMUGGLERS' GAME

BY THE DAWN of the nineteenth century, Cawsand, on the south-western edge of Plymouth, was a smugglers' paradise. Even today, it is not difficult to imagine the men, by moonlight, pulling their small boats onto the concealed beach, amidst the cluster of inns and cottages, stealthily unloading their contraband of brandy, salt and silk. Bent double, shuffling through the tunnels under the houses, their women stealing away the goods into fish cellars and storehouses, or keeping a watchful eye out for the customs officers who might suddenly arrive by sea to catch them in the act.

Although the scene may be romantic, this illegal 'free trade' – as the smugglers called it – was anything but: it was a lottery where the risks were high, the work was hard, and many a tedious night was spent in bitterly cold conditions. Success brought wealth, but at the cost of many lives and much toil.

After the devastation of the English Civil War, England was financially in ruins – thousands were homeless. Even by the Restoration of King Charles II,

the country still urgently needed money, and the age of the privateers returned. Of course, they hadn't completely disappeared during the Civil War: they were happily working for King Charles I raiding Parliament's naval forces all along the Devon and Cornish coasts.

After the war, Plymouth restored its beleaguered finances by stealing the wealth of other nations, ignoring any and all peace treaties. On 22 July 1660 two English ships entered Plymouth harbour, having commandeered three ships – one French, and two Dutch – laden with valuable trading goods and heading for La Rochelle. Another French ship, laden with wine and bound for Amsterdam, suddenly found itself 're-directed' to Plymouth, and its goods confiscated. Plymouth restored its fortunes by establishing its own 'pirate' economy.

Of course, Plymouth was also making money through legal trade with Europe and the New World, and Parliament took its own cut of this wealth by establishing taxes on all overseas trade – taxes that would rise to ridiculous levels to fund wars throughout the eighteenth and early nineteenth centuries. Customs officers were appointed in Plymouth, but their early efforts to control trade proved very unpopular. Goods that failed to pay the tax were confiscated, stored in great warehouses near the quay at Sutton Pool and often subsequently destroyed, much to the annoyance of the local population. In March 1679 the customs officers burnt illegally imported linen and canvas and staved in barrels containing 15 tons of French wine. The impoverished masses looked on in horror. In 1680, a further 30 tons of French wine, brandy and vinegar were dumped and French linen worth £2,000 was burnt.

Of course, the customs officers were not well paid and subsequently much of the contraband was never truly destroyed but simply disappeared. Customs officers were also notorious for taking bribes and stealing from ships. In 1595 Nicholas Halse, then controller of customs at Plymouth, was forced by the authorities to make reparations when the owner of the *Jewel* accused Halse of stealing valuable 'conchinella' and 'indico' from the *Jewel*'s hold. In 1614 the attorney-general was again accusing James Bagge, Plymouth's new controller of customs, of abusing his position.

By 1680, things were no better. The King sent his official, William Culliford, to Devon to investigate rumours of corruption amongst the customs officers, and Culliford was appalled to discover that the Plymouth officers were the most corrupt in the country, engaging in every kind of scam and larceny imaginable. The controller of customs at Plymouth was dismissed, and the service completely overhauled, but still the corruption continued.

No wonder then that smuggling became a major occupation in Plymouth and along the surrounding coastlines – corrupt officials, high taxes on imported goods, a lucrative trade with Europe just a short sailing distance away. The fishermen of Cawsand, skilled sailors and ship-builders all, saw an opportunity to make a little extra money, and took every advantage of the local conditions, knowing that, while the ships in Plymouth Sound were often stalled by southerly winds, Cawsand harbour was the ideal setting-off point into the Channel. The customs officers just couldn't catch them, even when they wanted to.

Soon, inns around Plymouth became storehouses for contraband – spirits, sugar, tobacco, and coffee. Even a church was a viable depot: Cawsand's local vicar was showing the rural dean around the top of the church tower at Maker church when he looked down to see twenty-three tubs of illegal spirits stored in the gutters. A tub of spirits left on the church doorstep the following morning bought the vicar's silence. While they benefited, the community simply kept quiet – and enjoyed a good drink to boot.

In 1747 the mayor, aldermen and merchants of Saltash complained to the lords of the Treasury that smuggling was becoming a major impediment to legal trade. The River Tamar was overrun with smugglers, all making use of the creeks and inlets around the Tamar to land their goods illegally. The mayor requested additional customs officers and searchers, but the Treasury refused the request, expecting Plymouth to foot the bill – which it didn't. Plymouth was making too much money out of smuggling.

And so smuggling increased in scale and daring. By 1780, 17,000 casks of spirits

The Tamar River near Saltash, infamous haunt of smugglers. (LC-DIG-ppmsc-08788)

were being landed each year at Cawsand. The risks were enormous and the money to be made incredible. From a little 'money on the side' for peaceful fishermen, the trade developed into a war of the sea – and it soon became a very bloody battle.

On a dark night in 1785 the *Happy-Go-Lucky* and the *Stag*, two smuggling vessels just returned from Guernsey, were quietly landing their cargo on the west of the Rame peninsula when the customs' boat *Pylades* discovered them. A midshipman of the *Pylades* secretly boarded the *Stag*, carrying a musket, but was spotted and the alarm was raised. As the *Stag*'s captain came up on deck, carrying a blunderbuss and preparing to defend his ship, the *Pylades*' midshipman opened fire – and blew a hole in the captain's midriff. The smugglers then opened fire on the *Pylades*, killing one customs officer and wounding two more.

'Kill them all!' the smugglers cried. 'Don't let one go ashore to tell their story!'

The smugglers escaped, but they were captured the following year in Falmouth. Ironically, the *Stag* had formerly been a customs' boat, mounted with eighteen guns, but was sold as unfit for use – only to be bought by a boat-builder in Cawsand and refitted for successful smuggling.

Harry Carter's name became infamously linked with Plymouth Sound. While running his illegal cargo into Cawsand one night, his ship, the *Revenge*, was suddenly boarded by naval officers. He and his crew fought valiantly, unarmed, until a Navy officer beat Carter senseless with a cutlass. Harry staggered and collapsed to the deck, only to come to while the Navy officers were busy securing Carter's crew in the hold. The wind was blowing hard from the south east and the *Revenge* ran aground, giving Harry his opportunity to escape. He crawled, unseen, across the deck and, in incredible pain, pushed himself over the side into the shallow water to struggle ashore across the rocks.

In Cawsand Harry Carter's brother, Charles, had been on lookout and gathered a team together to search the shore for any of their associates who might have escaped. They spotted Harry, still in his huge coat, almost lifeless, collapsed on the shore. They managed to hide him in the village and a doctor was sent for. An unnamed wealthy investor then hid Harry for three months, and he eventually managed to return to Cornwall, having escaped the customs officers for good.

But the violence continued. On a moonlit night in 1790 the smuggling ship *Lottery* was off Cawsand, unloading contraband spirits worth £6,000 into small boats, when the *Hind*, a revenue cutter with boatman Humphrey Glynn aboard, suddenly came alongside. The crew of the *Lottery* fired at the customs' boat, blowing Glynn's face off. It seemed that Glynn had his back turned to the *Lottery* while manoeuvring his ship, and the musket shot entered the back of his head and exploded out through his face.

In the subsequent confusion the *Lottery* escaped, but the hunt for the killer continued for two years. Glynn had been a respected member of the local community, married to a girl from neighbouring Kingsand. His death was a tragedy. Eventually, a smuggler named one Thomas Potter as Glynn's murderer and Thomas was taken to London and hanged.

The smuggling trade involved the entire community at Cawsand, as a visitor at the end of the eighteenth century described:

We descended a very steep hill, amidst the most fetid and disagreeable odour of stinking pilchards and train oil, into the town.... In going down the hill... we met several females, whose appearance was so grotesque and extraordinary, that I could not imagine in what manner they had contrived to alter their natural shapes so completely; till, upon enquiry, we found they were smugglers of spirituous liquors; which they were at the time conveying from cutters at Plymouth, by means of bladders fastened under their petticoats; and, indeed, they were so heavily laden, that it was with apparent difficulty that they waddled along.

After the capture of Napoleon, there were hundreds of naval personnel suddenly out of a job, and they entered the lucrative smuggling trade. The Cawsand smuggling fleet was expanded in 1815, with a fleet of cutters capable of shipping 1,000 five-gallon casks from Holland and France, as well as cargoes of silks, salt and tobacco.

For the local government the situation had become serious, and in the 1820s Plymouth supplied fourteen new revenue cutters to augment the existing services. Public sympathies, however, still remained with the smugglers, who faced terrible hazards defying what were seen as unfair import taxes. On 26 October 1822 the *Royal Cornwall Gazette* reported that a Cawsand-rigged smuggling boat from France had been totally lost on the previous Wednesday night near St Michael's Mount. The report continues: 'we regret to add all the crew drowned'. Despite the violence, the smugglers were rarely seen as criminals but as local people whose skills as sailors and navigators were greatly admired. They were sorely missed if they died in the appalling gamble that was 'free trade'.

AD 1768

VOYAGES OF THE DAMNED

THREE TIMES CAPTAIN James Cook set out from Plymouth on voyages of discovery that would explore the Pacific, discover the eastern coast of Australia, confirm the existence of the Baring Strait between Russia and Alaska, and circumnavigate Antarctica (the first man to do so). His discoveries would transform our knowledge of the world and its species, and open up communications and trade across the globe. However, they would also lead to the establishment of one of the most brutal convict colonies, in Australia; destroy the lives of native peoples in acts of genocide he could never have foreseen; and bring about his own horrific death at the hands of cannibals.

In August 1768 Captain James Cook set out from Plymouth on the *Endeavour*, en route to Tahiti to observe the transit of Venus, measurements for which would help scientists determine the distance between the Earth and the Sun. He also had secret orders, never revealed until they were discovered in the Navy Records in 1928, to find the great south land, at that time only fleetingly glimpsed by explorers. His journey would be an incredible success, with the discoveries of New Zealand and

---

Sir Joseph Banks, the acclaimed botanist travelling with Cook on his first voyage, was unimpressed by the Australian Aborigines when he met them fishing in the mangroves and marshes around Botany Bay. He remarked that they were a dirty people, caked all over in smelly mud, even in their hair. Within hours of landing, however, Banks' party were suffering from terrible mosquito bites, one of his team eventually dying from a resulting infection. In his diary, Banks pondered why the natives seemed so unaffected by mosquitoes, foolishly failing to make the scientific connection between the Aborigines' smelly mud and mosquito repellent.

Captain Cook receiving offerings in the Sandwich Islands. (LC-USZ62-102228)

the eastern coast of Australia. His first stop at Rio de Janeiro did not go well, however, as the Portuguese Viceroy mistook them for pirates and temporarily imprisoned members of his crew.

Then, at Tahiti, his crew all caught syphilis.

Well, not quite all of them, and it proved not to be syphilis (though the symptoms were very similar). As the male European sailors explored the Pacific islands and grew intimate with the friendly islanders, especially the women, a venereal disease called yaws became endemic throughout the islands. If a sailor brought a cut or scratch into contact with the skin of an infected islander, a painless 'mother yaw' would spring out, looking somewhat like a wart. These would then burst out into

ulcerous lesions, and the disease would begin to eat into the bones, joints and soft tissues of the victims, particularly the nose. This was often eaten quite away, leaving a huge crater in the victim's face.

Cook himself was adamant that his group of explorers should always be friendly with the natives they met on their journeys, but so not friendly that they introduced sexual diseases to the native populations. Unfortunately there was little Cook could do to prevent it, as the islanders had already caught the disease from previous explorers and traders, and Cook's crew were just another of many to whom venereal diseases would be passed on. Soon yaws and other diseases would cause havoc through the Pacific Islands.

In 1787, the ships *Friendship* and *Charlotte* set sail from Plymouth carrying male and female convicts to join the First Fleet, which would form the first European settlement in Australia. The fleet carried a total of 1,044 people, which included 504 male convicts and 192 female convicts, as well as – all the more horrifying – 17 children of convicts. The First Fleet tried to establish a colony at Botany Bay, under the advice of Captain Cook, but found no fresh water there. The land was also poor, so they sailed further north and eventually landed in Port Jackson, now called Sydney Harbour. The resulting colony suffered great deprivations in their first years, desperate for supply ships which turned up much later than expected. The land around Sydney was not much more fertile than Botany Bay, and food was scarce for many years. The convicts working in the heat in heavy chains were brutally abused by their marine overseers. One of the worst early effects of the settlement was the accidental introduction of smallpox, which devastated the Aboriginal population.

In 1789 the friendly natives of Tahiti were the ruin of Captain Bligh, whose crew mutinied on the *Bounty*, preferring to remain in their Tahitian idyll rather than return to their miserable lives in England. Though Bligh's brutal discipline was blamed for the mutiny, his methods were in fact no worse than any other captain's – floggings and other punishments were regular occurrences aboard the naval ships. Order had to be maintained. Cook was renowned as a more liberal task-master than most, but even he had to punish his men for insubordination, though their behaviour was much improved by his determination to see them well-fed and disease-free.

Captain Cook, despite his more open-minded attitudes towards native peoples and his liberal treatment of the crew, had his flaws – he was prone to tetchiness and temper – and it was these flaws that led to his own death. In 1776 Cook set out from Plymouth on his third voyage, in his ships the *Discovery* and the *Resolution*, intending to explore the Baring Strait and investigate the possibility of a passage from the Pacific into the Atlantic around the northern coasts of America. En route, he discovered the Hawaiian Islands, and explored Easter Island and the northern coasts of America. In the islands of the Pacific, Cook was frequently hailed as a god, and, although usually coping with the rituals and the adoration with humility, there was more than a little hint in his final days that the admiration had finally gone to his head.

Landing in Kealakekua Bay in Hawaii, he and his crew were again hailed as gods – but as the gods consumed all the food the deprived natives were more than happy to see the ships sail away at last. Cook had outstayed his welcome. However, the *Resolution* had been poorly fitted and, within a week, Cook was forced to return to Kealakekua for repairs. The natives were not impressed to see them back so soon. Expecting something in return for their hospitality, a group of them took a cutter from the *Discovery*. They wrongly assumed that this would be understood by Cook and his crew as their fair due. It was a cultural misunderstanding that was to have catastrophic effects: tetchy in his old age, Cook rushed to the shore, determined to take the island's King hostage until the cutter was returned.

The King and his two sons were actually quite happy to come aboard Cook's fine ship, but the Queen, in tears, begged for the return of her family – and the watchful Hawaiians decided that enough was enough. Cook found himself confronted by an angry mob. Muskets were fired in the panic and a Hawaiian chief was accidentally killed. The native men, armed with spears and stones, threatened Cook. Cook himself fired two shots to dissuade any further attack. Stones rained down upon Cook's men, who retaliated with more shot. Then, as Cook turned to his men to demand they cease firing, one of the warring natives stabbed him in the back.

As his men retreated, Cook's body was left on the shore at the mercy of the locals, who tore it apart. While the crew watched from their ship, unsure how to proceed, Cook's mutilated body was afforded a fine native funeral: it was dismembered, cooked and the pieces distributed amongst the natives. Captain Clerke, who assumed command, then had the grisly task of trying to collect the remnants of Cook's body, so that a 'proper' sea-burial could be performed.

Realising that the death was not an act of war but desperation, Clerke very wisely ordered that there be no retaliation against the natives, who, once calmed, were very sorry for the death of a man they had admired. One of the Hawaiian priests came on board to offer Clerke a tribute – a disgusting bundle of burnt flesh wrapped in cloth. Although they ritually dismembered the body, the story that the Hawaiians were cannibals is proved untrue by Clerke's diaries. The natives were asked if they had eaten any of Cook's body – a very difficult discussion requiring delicate translation. Clerke recorded that the islanders were horrified by the thought; when they realised what the captain was asking, they denied it hotly. Pieces of Cook's body were merely to be distributed as powerful tokens, not for human consumption.

Unfortunately, Captain Clerke then fell ill. During his incapacitation, a number of natives were slaughtered by the angry crew, their houses burnt to the ground. Suing for peace, the Hawaiian chiefs finally returned to Clerke a series of gruesome peace offerings – the head, hair and limbs of Captain Cook, for burial at sea.

Great Scott
Captain Cook may have died in the warmth of Hawaii, but his previous voyage had been a far chillier affair. Cook was dismayed

In 1803, Ann Croot was sentenced to seven years' transportation to Australia for stealing a shawl, a mason's hammer and a trowel, but the inspector of convicts refused to put her on board the ship, alleging that age and weak health meant she would die en route. On 9 January 1804, she was pardoned.

by the prospect of the frozen waste that was Antarctica. On his second voyage, leaving Plymouth in 1772, he described in his diaries 'the inexpressible horrid aspect of the Country; a Country doomed by nature never once to feel the warmth of the Sun's rays, but to lie forever buried under everlasting snow and ice.' He felt that 'whoever has resolution and perseverance to [proceed] farther than I have done, I shall not envy him the honour of the discovery but I will be bold to say that the world will not be benefited by it.'

Just 140 years later, Plymouth-born Robert Scott would be the man to prove Cook wrong in his assumptions, though Scott and his men would die in the attempt. March 2012 was the 100th anniversary of the death of Captain Scott and his men in the Antarctic. His final farewell letter sold for over £160,000 at auction in London, in which he pledged he and his team would together 'die like gentlemen'. The letter was written on 16 March 1912, as his men succumbed to starvation and hypothermia in a blizzard, just 11 miles from a food depot.

Robert Falcon Scott was born at Milehouse in Plymouth – a plaque there commemorates his links with the city. In January 1912 he led an expedition to be the first to the South Pole, but they were beaten by Norwegian explorer Roald Amundsen by just one month. Scott and his team

The doomed Terra Nova *expedition at the South Pole: Robert F. Scott, Lawrence Oates, Henry R. Bowers, Edward A. Wilson, and Edgar Evans. (LC-USZ62-8744)*

James Cook died and was buried at Ford Park Cemetery in Plymouth – not James Cook, famous captain of the *Endeavour*, but the dock worker James Cook, who was killed in an explosion on 13 December 1893 at Sutton Pool.

The *Standard* reported on 23 January 1894 that James and his colleagues had been working on deepening the harbour, which involved using a wrought-iron pipe to place explosives on the seabed; this was used to break up the rock so that dredging could commence. The top of the pipe was placed level with the dock and the explosives pushed down into the pipe using a long pole. Tragically, it seems that thick clay from the seabed glued the explosives to the end of the pole. As the pole was brought back up, the explosives came back up with it. Then the dynamite exploded, killing two dockworkers, including poor James Cook. A verdict of accidental death was recorded.

perished in the Antarctic wasteland, in temperatures of -40 degrees Celsius – it was freak weather even for the Antarctic, the winter unexpectedly arriving hard and early. Their frozen bodies were not discovered until February 1913, and a memorial to his enterprise was erected on Mount Wise.

But the enterprise was more than just a race to the South Pole. Scott was a dreamer, an adventurer, but also he was an explorer, just like Cook. For Scott, this Antarctic wilderness was a final frontier to be documented and discovered in all its harsh beauty. Although their mechanical sledges failed them and all their ponies had to be shot, unable to survive the bitter conditions, Scott's journey was one of remarkable discoveries. Scott and his team collected 2,000 specimens of animal life, including – for the first time – the eggs of the Emperor Penguin. His specimens are still the baseline by which the effects of chemicals and climate change are measured today. He was also the pioneer in the use of the camera for biological research. Even while struggling to return from the Pole, Scott took his men out of their way to explore a moraine near Mount Buckley, where he discovered fossils that proved the prior existence of the 'supercontinent' of Gondwana when the Antarctic lands had existed in a temperate climate. Scott became not only a legend and a tragic hero, but was also the founder of modern Polar science.

MUTINY!

IN THE MIDDLE of the wars against France, and the constant threat of a French invasion of England, the worst possible event occurred in 1797 – the British Navy went on strike. With the French Revolution and the publication of Tom Paine's *The Rights of Man* came an atmosphere of discontent aboard the ships, and a seaman's life was hard. They had not had a pay rise in 100 years. In fact, with the costs of the wars escalating, most sailors had not been paid at all for the previous two years. Barely 15 per cent of sailors were volunteers; the vast majority were conscripted or impressed, many as a result of being caught as smugglers. During the Napoleonic Wars, 103,660 deaths were recorded, 82 per cent dying from disease, 12 per cent in accidents or shipwrecks and only 6 per cent in enemy action. Combine this with the dreadful conditions on board and punishments such as flogging with a cat-o-nine tails, and it was no wonder that the Navy was an unhappy place of work.

In Plymouth, six Irish sailors had been hanged from the yard-arm for fermenting discontent. Suddenly there was news that the Navy ships at the Spithead and Nore anchorages had gone on strike. The Plymouth sailors cheered and raised the

---

In the eighteenth century women sometimes enlisted in the Navy, often to be near their lovers. Only breaches of discipline or sudden illness might mean discovery when they had to remove their clothes. In 1761, Hannah Whitney was in male attire when she was seized by a press gang and sent, with others, to work in Dock. She served as a marine and it was only to avoid flogging that Hannah finally revealed her sex. She had fought in many battles – and left the Navy whenever she felt like it, simply by resuming her normal attire.

Flogging aboard a man-o-war. (LC-USZ62-46517)

red flags, refusing to work. The Plymouth agitators were initially satisfied by a shilling a day increase and a promise not to make examples of the ringleaders, but petitions at Spithead went unheeded and Plymouth re-joined the strike, evicting officers from the ships. Suddenly, England's coastlines were undefended.

The mutinous crews then went a stage further: they attacked the officers that remained. Those officers who had mistreated their men were raised into the rigging on ropes, amidst cheers and jeers from their rebellious crews. Meanwhile the town, initially sympathetic to the sailors' plight, was given over to riot, and humiliated officers were paraded through the town and consigned to the Black Hole, a notorious prison on Fore Street. The houses of wealthy men were besieged (though the rioting achieved little more than hangovers and retaliation by the Navy, and was soon quelled).

The Navy retaliated in force. Lord Keith demanded the delivery of fifty of the most active mutineers or the punishment would include everyone. After quashing some further rebellion, Keith saw to it that fourteen men were condemned to death. Many others received 100 lashes apiece.

Meanwhile, there were rumours that enemies of the government had entered the Navy with the sole purpose of causing the disruption. One of these was an attorney called Lee, a rebellious man and a member of the United Irishmen, a Republican revolutionary group influenced by the American and French Revolutions. Lee joined the Navy, but it was soon discovered that he had enlisted with the object of spreading sedition. A drummer boy, sleeping under a hedge near Stonehouse, overheard conversations between Lee and his marine colleagues in which they pledged to start a treasonable uprising

In the mid-1700s, a young grenadier was sentenced to 500 lashes for desertion. He appealed and the sentence was duly changed – he was ordered to be shot. He was taken onto the Hoe before his assembled garrison, forced to kneel for the last sacrament, and then, at the very last moment, the King's Pardon was announced, to the cheers of all.

Hanging from the yardarm.

and free all the French prisoners. They vowed not to rest until 'they had overturned the government'. The boy alerted the officials at Stonehouse Barracks, and Lee and his comrades, Coffy and Branning, were tried and sentenced to be executed.

An old soldier called John McGennip, who, it was claimed, had encouraged Lee's plans, was mercilessly flogged on Plymouth

Hoe in front of the vast crowd, before being prepared for departure to Botany Bay. Then Lee, Coffy and Branning emerged from the Citadel. A marine band led the condemned party onto the Hoe, playing Handel's *Dead March* and accompanied by the three coffins held aloft. The three men were lined up and forced to kneel on their own coffins, and then the firing party approached.

Coffy and Branning fell at the first volley, but Lee remained untouched. One of the firing party then walked up to Lee with a loaded revolver. Placing the muzzle at Lee's ear, he blew off the top of his head.

Hundreds of troops were then paraded around the corpses in silence, as a warning to all who attempted sedition, and thousands then followed the procession of filled coffins to the Citadel. A contemporary account describes the procession as 'one of the most awful scenes the human eye has ever witnessed'.

AD 1799

THE BREAD REBELLION

WHILE HORATIO NELSON was famously fighting the French Revolutionary Wars, Britain was in turmoil. In 1799 the crops of wheat and barley, and then potatoes in Cornwall, failed, and with the wars in Europe, imported cereals became very expensive. The price of bread inflated beyond the ability of the majority of people to pay for it. Riots broke out across the country. Bakers' shops became battlegrounds as people desperately haggled over prices. In September 1800 the crops failed again, prices rocketed – and all hell broke loose.

By March 1801 the people of Plymouth were starving. In the three towns of Plymouth, Stonehouse and Dock (later called Devonport), there was a population of 47,000, with 3,000 people working at the Royal Dockyard; a high concentration of urban workers requiring enormous amounts – 220 bushels a week – of barley and wheat. With the failure of the crops, grain became expensive and the Plymouth Corporation valiantly tried to provide subsidies for the poor, but only managed this through the winter. By March, grain became like gold dust. Wars in Europe meant imported grain was no cheaper.

The Government tried bread substitutes – the failure of the potato crop not really helping matters – but the population were unimpressed at the prospect of imported herring for breakfast. By March 1801, there was less than 48 hours' worth of staple foodstuff in stock in Plymouth. The area simply ran out of food.

Many throughout the country, including some Plymouth magistrates, thought that the scarcity was an attempt by hoarding farmers to inflate prices. There was possibly some truth to this rumour, as the farmers could get very high prices indeed if they transported their grain to London. On 23 March, a protest started in Exeter: a mob of 300 attacked the local farmers, threatening a lynching if they didn't lower their prices.

On 30 March, it was Plymouth's turn. A mob gathered in Plymouth, and prices were reduced in the market the following day; Plymouth's farmers went in fear of their lives. However, the bakers refused to comply, and the mob started smashing windows.

One Plymouth baker was a member of the Volunteer Cavalry and successfully faced down the crowd with a drawn sword, but the protesters became so unruly that troops were called in – 1,400 militia in Plymouth and seventy cavalry from Dock (Devonport). The cavalry charged.

Two women and a dockyard worker were arrested, but the unrest continued. The highly organised dockyard workers went on strike in protest at their colleague's arrest, coming out of the yard 'in a body, whooping and huzzaing'. They were met with a troop of the Queen's bayonets, the pickets of the Wilts and East Devon and four loaded cannon. The Dockyard Committee demanded the release of the prisoner – and they got it, the magistrates siding with the people and releasing the dockyard protestor. The Committee also got the butchers and bakers to agree to set lower prices.

However, the bakers reneged on the deal and sent corn east to get higher prices. London received word of the dangerous precedents being set in Plymouth, and sent Lord Lieutenants Poulett and Fortescue to enforce the 'free market'; no price fixing by the dockyard workers would be tolerated. Colonel Bastard – yes, you read that correctly – of the South Devon Militia confiscated the side arms of any volunteer soldiers, and brought in professional troops to patrol the streets.

But the free market did nothing to prevent starvation, and soon the people of Plymouth, Stonehouse and Devonport were out again in protest. Rumours that a Devonport baker was hoarding sixty sacks of flour led to the mob attacking and robbing his shop. This attack lowered prices in the market again, but the troops, as before, made an arrest that led to a riot: Charles Jacob was taken up for smashing

Food riots broke out across the country in 1799. (With the kind permission of the Thomas Fisher Rare Book Library, University of Toronto)

Market Day in Taunton. A hundred years before this peaceful scene was captured, residents watched in horror as two men were executed here for their part in the bread riots. (LC-DIG-ppmsc-08886)

a window, whereupon the enraged crowd broke into the courthouse with battering rams and forced his release. Jacob was hidden away in the dockyard while the crowd smashed the magistrate's windows. (Ironically, the magistrate was St Aubyns, a major brewer dependent himself on a good supply of grain.)

During Jacob's rescue from the courthouse, two dockyard workers were arrested and the protesting mob on the street just got bigger. To be fair to the mob, they were protestors, not criminals – one fellow who stole a bag of potatoes during the turmoil was attacked, captured and handed over by women in the mob.

Troops locked the gates at the dockyard in an effort to starve out the protestors. However, they couldn't blockade the port, and some dock men sailed up the Yealm on 23 April. There they threatened the farmers again, forcing them to sell corn at reduced prices. A gunboat eventually captured and arrested the party, but by then a criminal gang had got in on

the act and attacked Honey's farm near Plympton, causing irreparable damage. Two of the gang were subsequently tried in Exeter and executed.

The authorities knew that something had to be done. The Navy Board reached Plymouth in May 1801 and sacked sixty-eight dockworkers: seventeen blacksmiths, twenty-two shipwrights, eleven labourers, six carpenters, three caulkers and three sailmakers, including all the union representatives who were on the Dockyard Committee which initiated the strikes. The butchers of Plymouth responded by raising the price of meat, declaring, 'that they shall do what they like now the Dockyard men are silenced'.

To quell further outbreaks of unrest in the South West, two men in Taunton, Samuel Tout and Robert Westcott, were sentenced to death for their involvement in the riots and executed in the middle of the marketplace. The subdued crowd watched in horrified silence. There were no more riots.

THE NAPOLEON EXHIBITION

IN 1815 NAPOLEON arrived in Plymouth. The Battle of Waterloo finally ended the war with France and the Emperor Napoleon Bonaparte, a military genius and dictator, was taken prisoner. In July 1815 the HMS *Bellerophon* (known to most as the 'Billy Ruffian') sailed into Plymouth Sound with Napoleon on board, on his way to exile on the Atlantic island of St Helena. To the British he was an unimaginable tyrant, and yet here he was in the flesh, seemingly benign. Thousands of small craft flocked to the Sound to catch a glimpse of the Emperor as he strolled on the deck, amused by all the attention and willingly posing for excited onlookers.

This engraving is based on the famous Eastlake painting: it shows Napoleon in his uniform, as approved by the man himself. (LC-DIG-pga-02908)

In the old Freedom Fields Hospital, a third-year student nurse once spotted a short man in a blue uniform running down a staircase. Security reassured her it was just the resident ghost of a Napoleonic prisoner of war.

AD 1625-1645

Under Siege

———◆◆◆———

RELATIONS BETWEEN
ENGLAND and Spain broke
down once again as King
Charles I came to the throne. Failed
plans for his marriage to a Spanish
princess brought only humiliation and
Charles subsequently declared war on
Spain. His father King James I had left
the country in a financial mess, and now
was Charles' chance to recapture some
of that wealth, but the wars brought
only death, disease and deprivation to
his naval port of Plymouth.

In 1625, ninety ships and 10,000
soldiers mustered in Plymouth Sound,
inadequately equipped and ill-fed. The
monies raised to support the troops
had been embezzled away by the naval
administrator, Sir James Bagge, who
lived at Saltram House. To make matters
worse, plague raised its ugly head again,
and Plymouth could not afford the cost
of boarding all these men. Many of the
soldiers were left starving and without
lodgings, stealing just to stay alive.

King Charles inspected his troops
on Roborough Down in a carnival

King Charles I. (With the kind permission of the
Thomas Fisher Rare Book Library, University
of Toronto)

atmosphere, plumes waving over
his beaver cap. However, he failed to
notice just how ragged and rebellious
his army was. Under the leadership of

The crew of the *Amersfoot*, a Dutch vessel moored in Plymouth Sound, were charged with barbarous cruelty. They watched and followed a group of English shipwrights leaving work at the Cattewater dock and then attacked them with swords. The fighting swelled as Dutch sailors and English dockmen joined the riot, with pistols and cutlasses. One onlooker was knifed to death. When challenged by the mayor, the Dutch cried that their attack was in response to the failure of King Charles I to keep his word with Holland. The King's foreign policies were tearing Plymouth apart.

Charles' court favourite, the Duke of Buckingham, the fleet sailed from the Sound. It sailed back, in terrible disarray, the moment the King departed, actually colliding with each other in the Cattewater. The fleet finally managed to get itself in order and sail, but it was not prepared for the mission ahead: it was hugely deficient in both ammunition and stores. Moreover, the Spaniards had been secretly forewarned of the attack.

The expedition was a failure. Many of the soldiers died of plague, food poisoning or exposure on the ill-equipped vessels. On the ships' return into the Sound, hundreds of putrid corpses were thrown into the harbour, and the narrow streets were filled with homeless soldiers, many wounded, and all stinking and diseased. Mass graves awaited them. The captains had to sell their stores to feed the sick, with no support coming from the King. James Bagge was vilified in Parliament, accused not only of embezzlement but of plundering a French vessel in Plymouth Sound to line his purse. Rumours spread that the monies went to the Duke of Buckingham, and to protect his friend, King Charles I dissolved Parliament to prevent his impeachment. Plymouth

joined Parliament in their censure of the King and his allies.

Buckingham then led a force to defend their protestant allies the Huguenots at La Rochelle, under attack from the French, but it was another disaster. The ill-fed and diseased soldiers mutinied in Plymouth and rebelled again when one of their number was sentenced to be hanged, the mob tearing down the gallows. At La Rochelle, as the ill-equipped English were forced to retreat, thousands drowned. Around 3,000 men, over half the expedition, were killed, and Buckingham's popularity plummeted to an all-time low. Again sick and wounded men were brought to Plymouth. The council issued an order to try to prevent them landing in Plymouth, but still the diseased men were brought ashore.

Battles between Parliament and the monarch came to a head in 1642, and civil war was declared. Cornwall sided with the King, while Devon sided with Parliament. At first, the administration at Plymouth was Royalist, under Governor Astley. However, the King made the terrible mistake of calling Astley to join him as a Major General in the Royalist army. The moment Astley departed, Mayor Francis and his Puritan allies took charge of Plymouth and declared it for Parliament. Although the rest of Devon and many ports around the country fell to Royalist forces as the war progressed, Plymouth remained the only port for Parliament throughout the Civil War, fiercely defending itself against the King in years of siege and hardship.

By 1642, Plymouth was a strongly walled town, with the fortifications built in the time of King Henry VIII still present on every headland around the Sound. The mayor decided that an outer line of fortifications was necessary, along the natural northern ridge that runs west to east from the old Stonehouse creek north of Mill Bay, to Lipson and Tothill – a line of about 4 miles that forms a crescent around the town. Every man, woman and child was forced to work to build the fortifications, digging trenches, building earthworks, and supplying the soldiers with ammunition, food and drink. 'Strong drink' was provided for when the fighting got bad – and it got bad.

Every man in Plymouth signed an oath to die in defence of the town rather than see it taken by the King, and as the Royalists took Devon, the people grew ever more desperate to defend themselves. Rumours circulated of what happened to the inhabitants as other besieged towns fell to the Royalists – horror stories of children slaughtered, women raped and men sold into slavery. These may have been exaggerated, but they also contained a kernel of truth.

Soon the Plymothians were hemmed in by Royalist troops at Saltash, Plympton and the headland now called Mount Batten, and Plymouth became increasingly isolated. Refugees from across the South West, fleeing the King's forces, arrived in great numbers in Plymouth, swelling the already overcrowded town to a population of 10,000. Living conditions inside the town soon became unbearable, with only the port able to supply food and fuel to the trapped inhabitants.

The King's men blocked the leat from Dartmoor that provided Plymouth with its fresh water, and plague and typhus soon flared up. Firewood became unobtainable. Yet they refused to surrender.

Warships at the time of the English Civil War. Ninety mustered in Plymouth Sound in 1625. (With kind permission of Thomas Fisher Rare Book Library, Library of Toronto)

1643 siege map of Plymouth, by Wenceslas Hollar. (With the kind permission of the Thomas Fisher Rare Book Library, University of Toronto)

When a Royalist trumpeter arrived at the town with a request from the King's forces for their surrender, he was whipped, beaten, imprisoned overnight, and then sent back with instructions never to visit the town again.

Plymouth was populated by men of military expertise and daring, often fuelled by Puritan passions. Repeatedly they led enthusiastic raiding parties beyond the line of forts to take on the Royalists.

Aware that the Royalists had established their headquarters at Modbury, east of Plympton, Colonel Ruthven, a Puritan of the Plymouth militia, mounted a bold plan. Ruthven took 300 mounted men north and then east, circumventing the motley Royalist army in Plympton and, in the mists of dawn, took the Modbury headquarters by complete surprise. With swords and pistols, Ruthven's men charged on Modbury, hitting the Royalist command post with such force that the 900 Royalists posted there immediately scattered. The Royalist senior officers, holed up in a local mansion, surrendered when Ruthven ordered his men to set fire to nearby outbuildings, the flames and smoke heading for the main house.

While Ruthven's fervent Puritans desecrated the local church, removing all 'heretical' images and iconography, the Plymouth forces captured the senior Royalist officers. Ruthven's genius was then to draw the remaining Royalist army – regrouping now for a counter-attack – to follow him east to Dartmouth, while the majority of the prisoners and Ruthven's men actually travelled west to Plymouth through Plympton. Splitting the party had the Royalists fooled, and Plymouth triumphed with the largest cache of Royalist senior officers ever captured.

Over the four years of the siege, there were many of these little victories, but the greatest victory for the Plymouth forces was to come with the Sabbath Day fight.

Prince Maurice – nephew to King Charles I and a man renowned for his atrocities against civilians in the wars in Europe – had been put in charge of breaking the siege at Plymouth. To defend their eastern borders, the Plymouth forces had built a new earth-work called Laira Point, overlooking the tidal Laira Creek that ran into the Plym. Laira Creek ebbed and flowed through a deep valley on the other side of the steep north-eastern ridge, but Prince Maurice saw this as a suitably weak target to break the siege.

He couldn't have chosen a worse location to attack.

In the dark, the lonely sentinels at Laira Point were engulfed. Suddenly Royalist forces were upon them, surrounding them from every side at once, and putting the Parliamentary supply ships moored in the Plym River at great risk. Hearing the alarm, however, Plymouth mustered its forces to retake Laira Point: unseen in the darkness, they approached the fort from the south, at Tothill Ridge, with a surprise counter-attack. Now it was the Royalists' turn to be surprised: the raiders suddenly found themselves under attack by 150 mounted defenders. However, despite this initial victory, the Plymouth forces broke under pressure, and they were forced to retreat west to Lipson Fort, near Freedom Park. Captain Wansey of Plymouth was shot in the fierce fighting.

The Royalists, spurred on by their triumph, charged west to take the town, but the Plymouth forces unexpectedly regrouped and 'swept all before them like a roaring torrent'. The King's men retreated, only to discover that the tide had turned behind them and now the Laira Creek was impassable. Trapped against the deepening rush of water, Maurice and his men floundered on the

---

A strange ghost from the English Civil War still haunts the Mount Gould Hospital, located near the line of forts once attacked by Prince Maurice in the Sabbath Day fights. After many strange occurrences, one male member of staff reported seeing a white lady in a patient's room. As he watched, the white lady disappeared through the wall. Though the patient in the room was well that day, he was dead by morning.

Plymouth Sound, showing the Civil War fortifications in 1646. (With the kind permission of the Thomas Fisher Rare Book Library, University of Toronto)

ridge overlooking the Laira, their horses plunging into the mud, riders riddled with shot from the attacking Plymouth forces. Hundreds of the Royalists died, drowning, sliding down the steep embankments into the muddy waters. At this point they were also targets for the ships still in the Plym estuary and many of the King's men fell into the hands of the Plymouth fighters. For many centuries, Plymouth's victory – the 'Great Deliverance' – was celebrated on 3 December, and with a commemorative monument at Freedom Fields.

In disgrace, Prince Maurice moved on, and in 1644 Sir Richard Grenville was appointed to oversee the siege on Plymouth. Again Sir Richard tried to intimidate the town into surrender, but his words were met with scorn. He had arrived late in the English Civil War after brutally attacking the rebellious Catholics in Ireland. Initially Grenville had declared himself for Parliament and had been appointed to lead an army to attack the King, but at the last minute he changed sides, taking his forces – and Parliament's money – with him to join King Charles. Grenville was branded the worst kind of traitor: a turncoat, 'skellum' and a rogue.

Grenville proved more sadistic and corrupt than even the Plymouth leaders could have imagined. Grenville became a war profiteer, kidnapping rich men in Devon and holding them in the horrors of Lydford Gaol until their families paid a large ransom; he thereby amassed a personal fortune in land and money. One story is particularly famous: while travelling between Plympton and Tavistock, Grenville and his party came upon four Plymouth soldiers gathering wood. Rather than take them prisoner, Grenville forced one of the Plymouth soldiers to hang each of his company from the nearest tree. Grenville then hanged the last man himself.

By January 1645, Grenville had had enough of fighting skirmishes with Plymouth's forces and launched a full-scale attack – with over 6,000 of the

Throughout the English Civil War, the gaol on St Nicholas' Island (now called Drake's Island) was used to imprison Royalist dissenters and traitors. After the Restoration, it was the turn of the anti-Royalists and non-conformers to be imprisoned there.

One such was Abraham Cheare, who was a pastor of Plymouth's Nonconformist Church and a victim of the religious intolerance that hounded Plymouth's inhabitants. In 1661, he was sent first to Exeter Gaol, charged with encouraging religious assemblies; he was then released in 1662, just as King Charles II removed 2,000 religious dissidents from their parishes (including the preacher for St Andrew's church in Plymouth). Cheare was imprisoned again in Exeter for holding unlawful assemblies. The conditions in Exeter Gaol were appalling and he spent many hours writing to his congregation telling them how he was relying on his faith to survive. His sister finally secured his release in 1665, but his return to Plymouth brought him back into the hands of his enemies, and he was held in the noxious prison near the Guildhall for a month before being banished to St Nicholas' Island, where he soon fell ill and died, aged just forty.

0056. - PLYMOUTH. PIER WITH DRAKES ISLAND.

Drake's Island in 1900, with the pier in the foreground. Prisoners were held on the island during the civil war. (LC-DIG-ppmsc-08786)

Hundreds of years later, the defenses can still be seen. (LC-DIG-ppmsc-08785)

King's men – against the central forts along the line. But the weather saved the city. The weather in Plymouth is notoriously wet in the winter months, and in January 1645 it didn't just rain – it rained for two days, a torrent that filled the ditches with water and made earthworks into mud. Again and again, Grenville sent in his forces to take the earthworks at all costs, only for his men and their horses to drown, sucked into the mud. When one of Grenville's own officers protested at the useless loss of life, Grenville ran him through with his sword.

Royalist cannon thundered through the night and at last Grenville's forces managed to take two of the forts along Plymouth's line of defences. However, Plymouth's soldiers battled on and killed sixty of Grenville's men at Maudlyn Fort, turning Grenville's own cannon against the oncoming Royalists.

At the fort of Little Pennycomequick, Grenville's men launched a trap: they somehow managed to take the fort, silently slaughtering every man inside. Then, quietly, they lay in wait, poised for their moment to take the town. But a Plymouth officer called Birch, approaching Little Pennycomequick, realised that the stillness inside the fort was not a good sign. He calmly approached the structure and someone within cried, 'Stand, who are you for?' Birch replied, 'for the Parliament' – and the rain of gunfire that responded told Birch the fort was taken. He instructed his soldiers to wait for Grenville's men to run out of ammunition. Then, while they were reloading, Birch and his men charged the fort. Hand-to-hand combat left the fort's walls and floor soaked in blood – and Plymouth victorious yet again.

The souls of over 100 French prisoners hanged in the Naval Dockyard still allegedly remain trapped in the oppressive atmosphere of the Hangman's Cell, which contains the last remaining working gallows in Britain. In the nearby Ropemakers' House, ghost hunters have sighted a phantom Victorian girl.

Charles Lock Eastlake, then just twenty-two years old, painted a portrait of Napoleon shown standing on the deck of the HMS *Bellerophon* while the ship was anchored in Plymouth Sound. The huge painting was based on sketches of Napoleon taken with the Emperor's permission: Napoleon himself even sent the artist parts of his uniform to ensure the painting's authenticity. Eastlake went on to become president of the Royal Academy.

In the confusion of post-revolutionary France, Napoleon was declared Emperor and his forces became a major threat to trade routes and the British Navy. In 1803 Napoleon formulated a plan to invade England, but the dying Admiral Horatio Nelson defeated the French Navy at the Battle of Trafalgar. Nelson had close ties with Plymouth, having been awarded Freedom of the City in 1801. Lieutenant John Pollard from Cawsand is still known as 'Nelson's Avenger', thought to be the man who killed the French sailor who shot Nelson.

After a series of humiliating military failures, including the disastrous retreat from Russia, Napoleon abdicated and was exiled to Elba, where he escaped and recruited French forces to take Paris. His ambitions came to an end in 1815 at the Battle of Waterloo.

England and her allies restored Louis XVIII to the French throne, and

Napoleon, escaped from Elba. (LC-DIG-pga-04089)

Napoleon once again became a prisoner, exiled to St Helena. There, in the damp accommodation, he eventually died of stomach cancer (though some say he was slowly poisoned).

During the Napoleonic Wars the French prisoners captured and held in Plymouth were poorly treated. Hundreds were hanged. Those imprisoned in the Citadel were whipped on arrival. The worst offenders went to the Black Hole, a noxious gaol on Fore Street. The remainder were held in appalling conditions, the prisoners complaining bitterly about the meagre food and decrepit cells. Sickness ravaged their numbers. Some of the prisoners gained extra food by corrupting the guards;

In an isolated corner of Stoke Damerel churchyard is the grave-stone of John Boynes, the markings indicating that he was Jewish and therefore buried apart from the others. The grave-stone reads: 'To the memory of John Boynes, late Stone Mason of His Majesty's Dock Yard, who was unfortunately drowned between the Island and Point returning from seeing Bonaparte in the Sound, 17th July 1815. Aged 35 Years.'

The grave of John Boynes.

this they sold on to their fellow prisoners in a black market.

In desperation, the French prisoners resorted to gambling to raise money for their keep, frequently losing their clothes in the process. During the worst winter months, French prisoners were seen naked on board the prison ships in Millbay, forced to sleep in rotting straw. Some were so weak from lack of food that they fell out of their hammocks and broke their necks.

In 1799 hundreds of French captives burrowed under the walls of Millbay Barracks and escaped. A 'hue and cry' was raised throughout the West and haystacks and outhouses were frantically searched for the famished and footsore soldiers. A number of merchant ships were discovered in the Sound deliberately concealing the wretched escapees, while two prisoners were found in a hotel in Honiton, having paid for a boat and a coach to get them there.

The Reel Cinema behind the modern Theatre Royal in Plymouth is haunted. It was built in 1938 over a graveyard containing the remains of Napoleonic prisoners of war. However, the ghost most frequently reported is that of a woman who sits in the front rows of screen two: during the film, she vanishes into thin air.

AD 1830

INVASION OF THE BODY-SNATCHERS

IN 1830 **THOMAS** Goslin and his pretty wife Louisa moved into Number 4 Millpleasant, a rather genteel address. Thomas Goslin, thirty-nine, was by all accounts a prosperous-looking man, a little short at 5ft 4in, with grey eyes and brown hair. He was known to wear expensive clothes, including a fine black coat. His wife was ten years younger, a tiny 4ft 11in and always well-dressed, and they brought with them three servants: Richard Thompson, his wife Mary and another man called John Jones (sometimes known as John Quinn), all in their twenties. The Goslins declared to their neighbours that they were delighted with their new home: so quiet, and in such a secluded area! They didn't seem to mind that it was so close to the walled graveyard of Stoke Damerel church.

Of course, they failed to mention that they were all notorious body-snatchers.

Body-snatching has a long history in Britain. As medical schools in London and Edinburgh swelled with students, so the need for fresh bodies increased. Each student needed at least three bodies to

practise surgery and to study anatomy. Meanwhile, the number of hanged felons decreased year on year as more convicts were transported to the colonies. This may still have been, in practice, a death sentence for many, but nonetheless it left the surgeons and students with fewer and fewer fresh corpses to study. In the very early days, desperate anatomists dug up the

Stoke Damerel church.

recently buried themselves, but in 1721 apprentice surgeons were legally forbidden from exhuming the dead. So many schools offered payment for a good supply, usually through intermediaries. They thereby established the gruesome profession of the 'resurrectionist'.

In the eyes of the law, a dead body had no value and did not belong to anyone. The theft of a body did not count as a felony, therefore, but as a misdemeanour – providing that no actual possessions were stolen at the same time. Heavy fines or short prison sentences were the most a 'resurrectionist' would expect if caught, so the trade was seen as a relatively safe one. It was also extremely lucrative: a body-snatcher could be paid anything from forty-two shillings to £14 for a fresh adult corpse, so a quiet graveyard became a goldmine to those prepared to get their hands dirty. Jewish bodies were particularly prized, their quick burials ensuring the deceased had not decomposed, though the difficulties of moving a body still in a state of *rigor mortis* had to be considered. Even a decayed body could provide a good supply of teeth to sell. The London Medical Schools quietly left a supply of sacks outside the door for their suppliers' use and never asked any questions.

Sir Astley Cooper was the most eminent surgeon of his day and regularly paid body-snatchers to help him with his research and to maintain his well-stocked museum of diseased body parts. When informed in 1820 that one of his former patients had died in Suffolk, Sir Astley set about retrieving the body for further study. Sir Astley had once performed surgery on the man and wanted to see how the ligatured blood vessels had fared in the intervening years, so he paid Thomas Goslin – at that time called Thomas Vaughan – to fetch him the corpse. Thomas and his associate were paid £13 and twelve shillings for their trouble, which included the cost of hiring a coach to transport the secretly exhumed body from Suffolk to London.

This was just the first of many corpses Thomas 'retrieved' for Sir Astley over a long career. He had come from Limerick to London with his family and as a youth had acquired a reputation as a ruffian. His first job as a stonemason's labourer in a graveyard told him that there was more money to be made in desecrating the graves than in maintaining them. However, his success in London brought him into violent conflict with another successful grave-robber, so he hastened to Kent and for some time sent bodies to London from there. Thomas and his associates were nearly caught in Maidstone with a cart containing the freshly exhumed bodies of two men, two women and a child (or a 'small', as they were known in the trade). The officers

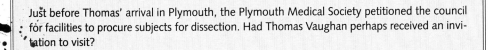

Just before Thomas' arrival in Plymouth, the Plymouth Medical Society petitioned the council for facilities to procure subjects for dissection. Had Thomas Vaughan perhaps received an invitation to visit?

who nearly apprehended them thought they were chasing smugglers, but were horrified to discover the stinking 'product' being smuggled.

Thomas fled Kent for Berkshire. By the time the Maidstone police caught up with him, he was serving three months in Reading gaol for stealing a body from a churchyard in Bray. On his release he was arrested again and taken back to Maidstone, where he promised to pay £100 bail – and promptly disappeared.

He then reappeared briefly in Sussex, it is thought, where he purchased a dead woman's body from her own husband and then established his trade again in Manchester and Liverpool. An old adversary informed the police of Thomas' whereabouts, and he finally stood trial in Maidstone for the five bodies found on the cart. Again he escaped, this time by sawing through the bars in the cell window and using his bed-sheets as a climbing rope.

Back in Manchester, his associates had been discovered in a stable, cramming corpses into 2ft-long boxes for transport. Even though his friends were in custody and he was on the run, Thomas still had the audacity to visit St Mark's churchyard to survey the prospects and ask the stone-cutter there about any funerals that day. The stone-cutter alerted local officials and sentinels were placed to try to catch the robbers. At midnight two men appeared and started digging – they were fired upon but escaped apparently unharmed.

A Maidstone constable, hearing of the event, then travelled to Manchester and apprehended Thomas while he was having his breakfast. Thomas tried desperately to escape but found himself trapped by the bars on a casement window. He spent two years in prison at Maidstone.

Thomas Goslin in action!

His arrest caused a national outcry, for when they examined the burial grounds in Manchester locals discovered 200 bodies had been stolen, never to be seen again.

Thomas was one of the ten best 'resurrection' men of his day, his work often undetected. He used all the best methods. Wooden shovels made less noise than metal ones. His 'dark lanthorns' shone only a narrow beam of light as his team dug a hole at the head of each grave and exposed just the top third of the coffin. Using the remaining earth on the coffin as a counter-weight, the snatchers ripped open the lid and with hooks pulled the corpse from the grave head-first. They stripped the corpse and left the clothes in the coffin – so as not to be caught as thieves, the penalty for theft being much more severe than that for stealing a corpse. The coffin was then covered over with the same earth. Thomas cleverly used cover sheets on the sides of the grave, so the surrounding earth would appear undisturbed.

Alternatively, his team would start a tunnel a few feet from the head of the grave, and break open the top of the casket, pulling the bodies with hooks all the way back up through the tunnel, never disturbing the earth over the gravesite at all.

Uninterrupted, the team could remove a dozen bodies in a night, piling them onto a cart for transport. The bodies were then packed into crates just 14in wide and deep, and 2ft long; a macabre courier service.

Women were vital to the body-snatching trade, though ironically it would be women who would end Thomas's career. The female accomplices would mingle with the mourners at the funeral, and ask questions about the condition of the deceased. They would also appear at workhouses, pretending to be relatives of the sick and dying. Once by the bedside, they would claim the corpse. A cart could then take the fresh body directly to the medical school for sale. They didn't come much fresher than that.

Of course, the trade created outrage amongst the grieving relatives and friends. To have paid for a decent burial only to have the body so desecrated was an abomination. Many still believed that, come the resurrection, their deceased needed to be intact. Only murderers, their souls already damned, were seen as fit material for anatomical dissection. Relatives paid small fortunes for secure tombs and rented mortsafes – locked iron cages that enclosed the coffin after burial, until the deceased had decayed sufficiently to be of no further interest to a bodysnatcher. Churches would hire out mortsafes and set up watch-towers over burial grounds, but the trade continued, unabated.

After being released from prison, Thomas established his trade again in Great Yarmouth. Calling himself Thomas Smith, he set up a house and stable and hired new accomplices. Then he paid the sexton of the local church, Jacob Guyton, to provide him with information on funerals. Soon, though, rumours began to spread of grave-robbings. Thomas was one for the ladies, and while trying to seduce a young local woman he seems to have let slip details of his trade.

Stoke Damerel churchyard was also the location of a wicked murder. In 1788, Philip Smith, a clerk from the Survey Office, was killed in the churchyard by a severe blow to the head. Eventually two murderers were caught: William Smith and John Richards, who had been seen together near the churchyard at the time of the murder.

Richards was a disreputable character who had been sacked from the dockyard and previously involved in numerous violent altercations. It seems William Smith had been offered payment if he helped Richards take his revenge against Philip Smith. Though they denied this, both Smith and Richards were sentenced to be hanged at Heavitree Gallows in Exeter and, by order of the judges, their bodies transported to a gallows at the edge of Stoke Damerel churchyard, by the creek once there, where their corpses would be kept hanging in iron cages until they had rotted.

It took seven years for the bodies to rot, pecked at by birds, blown apart in storms. The cage containing William Smith's body finally broke free and his body was then interred under the gallows, unmarked, while Richards' body simply disappeared, probably falling into the river and washing away. The gibbet itself rotted and fell into the river in 1827, and a local carpenter made a fortune making snuff boxes from its wood.

The chief of police informed the sexton – without realising that Guyton would then help Thomas and his associates to escape.

George Beck was a baker in Great Yarmouth, whose wife had sadly died in childbirth in October 1827. Concerned by the rumours, he anxiously uncovered his wife's coffin on 4 November. To his horror, he discovered that her body was gone; only her burial gown remained. He was devastated. Soon the cemetery was crowded with grieving townspeople searching for their deceased relatives, frantically digging out the graves and revealing that twenty bodies had been taken. One onlooker remarked that the churchyard now resembled a monstrous ploughed field.

The police eventually captured Thomas' accomplices, who quickly gave him up. On hearing of Thomas' arrest, the townsfolk turned into an angry mob. Labelled the 'monster fiend', Thomas needed a police escort to the courthouse. His old friend Sir Astley Cooper paid Thomas' bail and Thomas left the gaol disguised as a sailor to avoid the crowds baying for his blood. Sir Astley covered Thomas' expenses at the trial, and even paid Thomas' wife ten shillings a week while Thomas served six months in the gaol at Norwich Castle.

On his release, Thomas was immediately back in business – this time at the Red Cow pub in Colchester where police discovered three bodies, one of them a dead baby wrapped in a handkerchief. The grisly corpses had to be displayed for their grieving relatives to identify them. Thomas faced trial again, but was freed due to lack of evidence – no one had actually seen him exhume or transport the stolen bodies.

Thomas realised he needed to move to a new location, and saw Plymouth as a viable destination. Stoke Damerel church was ideal: it was secluded, surrounded by high walls, and received a regular supply of new bodies from the swelling population in Devonport.

And there was another bonus – ghosts! The townspeople did not like to walk past the churchyard, as it was thought to be haunted. A gibbet with a horrifying history had stood on the edge of the churchyard for many years and had only recently blown down. Also, the saucer-eyed ghost of a waterman had been seen, thought to haunt the churchyard because his widow had so quickly found herself a new husband.

All in all, it was an ideal location for nightly endeavours – and soon the dead of Devonport were in regular transit to the anatomy schools of London.

However, Charles' taste for young women would once again bring about his downfall. He was soon making advances to a pretty servant girl who lived across the road. She rejected him, and furthermore she informed her master that she did not trust the new neighbours. The suspicious master kept an eye on the newcomers and, after witnessing some strange behaviour, reported his suspicions to the police. The neighbour assumed that he had captured a ring of smugglers, but he was to find that his new neighbours were something much, much worse.

The head of the police, Richard Ellis, formerly a London Bow Street officer, decided to see these miscreants himself, and wandered into Stoke Damerel in disguise.

There he discovered Richard and Mary Thompson, alleged servants to Thomas Goslin, loitering in the churchyard, while two coffins entered the church. As he watched, Mary Thompson approached the mourners over each grave. Mary remained in the churchyard for a few more minutes before following her husband back to their residence at No. 4, Millpleasant.

Ellis realised something was wrong and, with remarkable intuition, decided to return to the graveyard that evening with his constables, James Day, Roger Halse, Ambrose Nosworthy and a fourth called Pike. Pike and Ellis hid in a north-east corner. After two hours of sitting in the dark, they heard someone digging in the graveyard, apparently from the spot where a body had been buried that day. Ellis saw a man wandering about, one who gave the appearance of being a look-out, but he could make out nothing more in the dark. Just before dawn, Ellis took his men to No. 4, where Ellis and Nosworthy climbed over into the back garden. Finding the back door locked, Ellis tried the window. Suddenly John Jones appeared, partly dressed. Ellis gave a plausible explanation – he said he was looking for deserters – while Nosworthy forced his way through the open window and past the servant. He then unlocked the back door, and the policemen entered the house.

The scene inside was sickening. Ellis found two sacks lying on the floor in the middle of the kitchen, a hole revealing at least one human body inside. In a kitchen cupboard they discovered a bag of human teeth; in the parlour, piles of grave-clothes. Here was the first – and last – mistake made by Thomas Goslin, and the great mystery of his capture. To steal the grave-clothes was theft, punishable by hanging or transportation. For the first time in all his years as a 'resurrectionist', he was caught stealing. Ellis and his men found the other body-snatchers still in bed – though Robert Thompson was in fact hiding *under* the bed and refused to come out; he was eventually dragged out by the police. As a final horror, the police made another macabre discovery: the nearby sink was full of teeth.

With the culprits locked up, Ellis searched the graveyard to confirm that the bodies interred just the previous day were in fact missing, and very likely were the two corpses now resting on the Goslins' kitchen floor. News of the grave-robbing reached the community, and suddenly there were hundreds of people in Stoke Damerel churchyard, all demanding to check that their deceased loved ones were still buried in the churchyard.

In all, nine bodies were found to be missing. Seven were never recovered. Many others had been disturbed, but left when found to be too decomposed. This didn't stop the 'resurrectionists' removing the heads, however, and the piles of teeth at the Goslins' house were proof that they were making a substantial income from this grisly haul alone.

The two bodies on the Goslins' kitchen floor were quietly restored to their graves. The first was that of an eighteen-year-old girl called Eliza Hanger from Devonport. The other was that of Thomas Webb, fifty-four, from Garden Street, whose corpse was still oozing from the sickness that killed him.

The Goslins and their staff had to be escorted under armed guard to Exeter, and entered the courtroom protected by double rows of constables – anything less would have seen them lynched. There the Goslins seemed unrepentant. An onlooker

Stoke Damerel churchyard is a quietly attractive though rather grim place now, the churchyard empty of bodies. In 1870, the graveyard was so overcrowded with coffins that some had actually broken the surface, and locals were complaining of the smell. The bodies were disinterred and moved to Efford Cemetery. The remaining gravestones were then laid flat into gruesome paving stones, forming an eerie path. The cracked and sometimes broken paving stones lifting away from the soil leave the visitor with the disturbing impression that the grave-robbers may never have departed.

Gravestones in Stoke Damerel churchyard.

pointed at Louisa Goslin and asked, 'has that woman been stealing bodies?' Louisa confirmed that she had – and declared that she would do so again, given the chance. In the nineteenth century a wife was rarely condemned for her husband's crimes – certainly this saved Mary Thompson from punishment – but on this occasion Louisa Goslin damned herself. Along with her husband and his two male associates, Louisa was found guilty of theft and sentenced to transportation for seven years to the settlement at Van Dieman's Land, now known as Tasmania, off the southern coast of Australia.

It may be that Thomas himself did not steal the clothes: he had always been very particular about leaving the grave-clothes in the coffin. However, evidence produced in court revealed that the pile of grave-clothes found in the kitchen may not have been the only clothing stolen during

the Goslins' career: one of the constables found a lady's shift on a chair in the back parlour, wet as though recently washed. Louisa tried to claim that it was hers, but Elizabeth Netting confirmed in court that her mother-in-law had been buried in that very item.

Thomas Goslin, John Jones and Richard Thompson were first sent to the prison hulk, *Captivity*, sitting in the Hamoaze, the estuary near Devonport. Unlike other prisoners, they were never taken off the ship to work on land in the gangs. The authorities knew full well that their lives would be in danger if the public spotted them. Louisa spent fourteen days of hard labour at Exeter Bridewell, eventually joining her husband and his friends on their way to the brutal convict colony in Van Dieman's Land. They served their sentences, took their punishments and lived on in the New World, never to return.

AD 1831

HUMAN TRAFFIC

I**N 1831, WHILE** his ship was being refitted in Devonport dockyard, Robert Fitzroy advertised that he was looking for a scientist to travel with him on his second surveying voyage to the Cape Verde islands and the coasts of South America.

Charles Robert Darwin, failed medical student and budding naturalist, applied – but was at first refused. Fitzroy was a committed Tory, who accepted slavery as a necessary evil, while Darwin was a Whig from a family of very active anti-slavery reformers. The two men would never get along.

As a phrenologist, a popular science of its day, Fitzroy believed that the appearance and structures of a man's face and skull determined his capabilities and his character. To Fitzroy, the inferiority of the African slave was a scientific matter. Fitzroy was unimpressed by the shape of Darwin's nose as well as his politics, but a mutual friend brought them together and Darwin was finally accepted on board Fitzroy's ship, the famous HMS *Beagle*, for a voyage that would change the world with Darwin's controversial

In May 1674, a slave called Joseph Bando ran away from his master's house on Mark Lane in Plymouth.

Joseph must have been an unusual sight. Slaves were an expensive luxury in Plymouth as most of the population could not afford £24 for a slave, though slaves did work farms in Tamerton Foliot for a while. So the sight of an escaped slave in Plymouth must have turned people's heads. Bando was tall, slender, about seventeen, a little disfigured by smallpox, wearing a blue livery coat and breeches, edged with white, with blue stockings and a gold wire in his right ear. A reward was advertised in the *London Gazette*, but whether the poor man was re-captured is not known.

Charles Darwin, who sailed from Plymouth.
(LC-DIG-ggbain-03485)

theories of evolution, the origins of man and survival of the fittest. It was also a voyage into the slave trade.

Throughout the 1700s, Plymouth ships continued Hawkins' notorious enterprise. The *Pindar* set out from Plymouth in 1707, and disembarked 285 slaves at Jamaica. In 1709 the *Joseph* deposited a further 280 slaves there. The civil leaders and merchants in Plymouth were active participants, calling for a repeal of taxes on any slave trading, and petitioning the House of Commons in 1710 for a free and open slave trade. The tax was eventually repealed, though mainly to the benefit of the ports at Bristol and Liverpool. In 1713 Britain became the leading slave-trading country, guaranteeing the delivery of 144,000 slaves to the Spanish Caribbean over the next thirty years.

As details of the horrific treatment of slaves reached the general public, however, the acceptance of slavery abruptly changed, both in Plymouth and across the country. In 1807 the abolitionists, Darwin's family included, finally succeeded in making it unlawful for any British citizen to capture or transport slaves, but the ownership of slaves was still commonplace throughout the British colonies, providing labour for the production of all those wonderful commodities – sugar, tea, coffee and cotton. The trafficking of human beings was banned, but not the ownership – which meant that slave ships still supplied the plantations, though now they came under attack from the British Navy. Between 1814 and 1828, public meetings were held in Plymouth desperately calling for a final end to all forms of slavery in Britain and all her colonies.

The atrocities Darwin witnessed in the countries visited by the *Beagle* would harden him against all forms of exploitation.

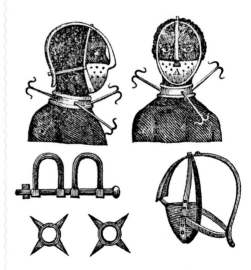

Torture devices used on slaves, as reported to Darwin: collar, gag and pronged neck collar.
(LC-USZ62-31864)

While waiting in Devonport, Darwin received word of the failure of his cause in Parliament. The Slavery Abolition Act was finally passed in 1833 while he was at sea.

Arriving in Bahia, Brazil, where 41 per cent of African slaves were landed, Darwin was appalled to discover that everyone he met who wasn't a slave owned at least one slave. As Captain Fitzroy was carried by slaves, in a sedan chair, into the town, Darwin roamed around the sweltering streets and discovered hundreds of slaves at work, and stories of horrific abuses – murder, and torture with gags, shackles and pronged collars. Escaped slaves frequently committed suicide, throwing themselves off cliffs rather than suffer re-capture.

Slaves carrying a sedan in Brazil, such as transported Captain Fitzroy. (LC-USZ62-97215)

It seemed that the restrictions on transporting slaves were only driving the slave trade underground and making it all the more brutal. In Montevideo, the *Beagle* came under the protection of the HMS *Druid*, who had just captured the *Destimida* secretly transporting slaves. The captain and men of the *Druid* had searched high and low for slaves on board, without success –until an officer thrust his sword into a water butt. A pained cry from within revealed that five slaves had been stored away inside that one barrel. Forty more slaves were discovered jammed into the crevices between the water casks under a false deck.

During the voyage, Darwin saw evidence to refute the accepted truism of savagism – that the black slaves were a sub-species of mankind who could not be civilised. The prevailing argument was that it was not cruel to treat these creatures as slaves, just as it was not cruel to domesticate and work a farm horse. In fact, Darwin had found many of the slaves themselves perfectly 'civilised', and went on to prove his theory that mankind was all of one species.

In the native tribes of Patagonia, Darwin met good-natured men and women with excellent abilities for languages. But these same people Captain Fitzroy regarded with horror, as 'animals' secretly capable of the worst barbarities. Fear, Darwin realised, was the primary source of racism,

---

In 1825, a slave woman escaped Jamaica and made her way to England – ironically landing first in Plymouth, Hawkins probably having transported her ancestors to Jamaica. Once in Plymouth, though, she was granted her freedom.

---

leaving the white traders seemingly oblivious to their own barbarities against black slaves.

Even after the Slavery Abolition Act of 1833, slavery issues still fermented debates, with slaves still working the fields in the southern states of America. Dr Charles Caldwell from Kentucky was a visiting speaker at a meeting of the British Association for the Advancement of Science in Plymouth in 1841, with Charles Darwin in the audience. (It is thought that Richard Owen announced his discovery of the dinosaurs at the same meeting.)

The bombastic, slave-owning Caldwell refuted Darwin's claims of the common origins of man and was determined to convince his audience that the black African was closer in appearance and intelligence to the higher forms of apes than mankind. Only whites, Caldwell believed, had any capability for culture. The science of ethnology, supported by Darwin's former host, Captain Fitzroy, was still ranking and dividing the races rather than unifying them, a dangerous precedent for the racist propaganda that would sweep through Germany before the Second World War.

FIRE AND TEMPEST

JUST **10 MILES** south of Rame Head is the Eddystone, a jagged reef mostly submerged at high tide, which has claimed countless lives in horrific ship-wrecks over the centuries, ships literally sinking without a trace.

It was here, in 1700, that Henry Winstanley, a renowned dreamer of humble origins, achieved the impossible. It had taken him four years in stormy condi-tions, but he managed to build the first lighthouse on the slimy rocks at Eddystone. In just a few short years, its shining light saved hundreds of ships. But the Plymouth coast is notorious for gales, especially in the winter months, and November 1703 brought the worst storm ever to hit the southern shores. As the tempest ravaged Plymouth, smashing houses and wrecking ships, Winstanley defiantly remained in his lighthouse to finish some repairs. On the shore, the light from the Eddystone was still seen until midnight, flickering in the ferocious gales, but by the morning it was no more; only a few twisted iron beams remained rising from the bedrock. The lighthouse, with Winstanley still inside it, had been swept out to sea.

Subsequent lighthouses fared little better. Rudyerd's Lighthouse, built of wood in 1709, was consumed by fire. As the lighthouse burned, the keepers clung to

Mr Jones was the keeper of the lighthouse on the Breakwater, an astonishing construction built to calm the waters of Plymouth Sound. In January 1845 Mr Jones' body was discovered on the Breakwater below the lighthouse. He had fallen to his death. Previously there had been horizontal iron rods around the lighthouse, constructed to allow work to go on above the tides. But the lighthouse keeper, deciding that they were no longer necessary, had just had them removed. If the iron rods had still been there, they would have broken his fall.

The Eddystone Lighthouse. (LC-DIG-ppmsc-08791)

the Eddystone rocks, desperately awaiting rescue. One of the keepers, Mr Hall, looked up – and met a horrible fate when molten lead from the lighthouse dripped down his throat. Some stories say that when he died, aged seventy-five, a ball of lead was discovered in his stomach.

Subsequently Smeaton's Lighthouse, despite its excellent design, was undermined in 1877 – quite literally, as the water had eroded the rocks beneath it. The top of Smeaton's Lighthouse now stands proud on Plymouth's Hoe, a shrine to the god-like powers of wind, fire and water.

Shipwreck!

In 1796, before the construction of the Breakwater, a gale hit Plymouth with such incredible fury that the *Dutton* was wrecked.

The ship had been making for shelter in the Cattewater, through monstrous waves and heavy rain, when she hit a shoal of rocks near Mount Batten and lost her rudder. Bereft of control, she crashed onto the rocks beneath the Citadel.

The *Dutton* was carrying 400 soldiers and many women and children: 500 people crowded onto the deck, desperately trying to escape as the waves crashed over them. The guns of the Citadel boomed out, calling for rescue, and a rope was cast from the shore – one end attached to a bolt on the ship, the other held by fishermen on the banks. Each passenger clung to a slippery iron ring and was pulled through the raging surf – half-drowning in the process, as the sea was starting to carry off the wrecked ship.

Amidst the chaos and confusion, Captain Edward Pellew of the Royal Navy, on shore, called for volunteers to board the *Dutton* and assist the passengers. From a terrified crowd only one man volunteered, a midshipman called Edsell. Pellew grabbed the iron ring and was dragged through the waves to the ship and immediately took charge, threatening to run through with his sword anyone who disobeyed him.

Meanwhile, the brave Mr Edsell came alongside the *Dutton* in a small boat to bring two more ropes, increasing the flow of passengers transported to safety, starting with the women and children. A master attendant from the Royal Dockyard also managed to bring a larger boat alongside and saved hundreds of lives, as Pellew firmly calmed the panicking passengers (and knocked down some drunken soldiers who threatened anarchy). It seems that the ship's officers, in the panic, had given up any hope of saving the passengers. Pellew was therefore forced to take command.

With the water rising over the deck, Pellew swiftly turned anarchy into order. He himself saved a three-week-old baby after reassuring the distraught mother that the child would be safe in his care. Only after the last of the passengers was safely on shore did Pellew and Edsell escape, leaving three crewmen to release the rescue ropes.

Total disaster was averted, and the number of casualties reduced from four hundred to fifteen. The heroic Captain Pellew, just twenty-nine, was awarded the Freedom of the Borough and knighted by the King.

However, the same year brought further disaster – but this time the casualties were far higher. The frigate *Amphion* had pulled into Plymouth for repairs and was hosting a farewell dinner for the crew, who were preparing to sail the following day. The ship was crowded with soldiers, their sweethearts and families, most from Plymouth. Over 300 people were on board, more than the usual compliment.

Their festivities turned suddenly to terror: the masts lifted, as though they were forced upwards, and the hull immediately sank. The sea boiled and hissed as flames shot up and then subsided. In Plymouth it felt like an earthquake. The sky reddened with a spray from bloodied and broken limbs, and headless bodies suddenly littered the deck. Heads blackened by gunpowder splashed into the sea like cannonballs. William O.S. Gilly published an account of the tragedy in 1864:

> Strewed in all directions were pieces of broken timber, spars and rigging, whilst the deck of the hulk, to which the frigate had been lashed, was red with blood, and covered with mangled limbs and lifeless trunks, all blackened with powder.

The frigate had been originally manned from Plymouth, and as the mutilated forms were collected together and carried to the hospital, fathers, mothers, brothers and sisters flocked to the gates, in their anxiety to discover if their relatives were numbered amongst the dying or the dead.

In the dining room Captain Israel Pellew had been thrown off his seat by the first explosion, but by some force of instinct he and his first lieutenant rushed to the cabin window before the second explosion blew them into the water. They were lucky to survive. The boatswain on the deck was blown off his feet and recovered consciousness only to find himself tangled amongst the rigging, his arm broken. Fortunately he had a pocket knife with him, and cut himself free.

Of the 300 on board, only eleven survived. One survivor was a child whose mother had held him in her arms to protect him as the explosion hit them both. The force tore her body in half, but still her arms were clasped around him as he was pulled from the wreckage. She never let go. The child was taken into care and joined the Navy, where it is said he had a successful career.

As the wreckage was scoured for survivors, the relatives on shore were faced with the task of identifying their loved ones from the bags of limbs and carcasses brought to land. Body parts were washed ashore with every tide.

As to the cause, the discovery of a sack of powder established the theory that a gunner, probably drunk, accidentally dropped some powder whilst attempting to steal from the stores. This ignited, and in its turn caught the main magazine. The thieving gunner died in the blast.

In 1824, 'The Great Storm' hit Plymouth, decimating the south coast and ripping 200,000 tons of stone from the Breakwater. The ferocious seas and gales threw boats around like matchsticks, with over twenty boats driven ashore. The gunners from the Citadel set out on the stormy harbour and rescued 200 mariners from the stricken vessels in the Sound.

Fire and Ash!

In 1836 an accidental fire at the house of Major Watson at the Citadel proved fatal. The family and the household retired to bed about 1 a.m., but a servant had left some wood on the extinguished fire to dry overnight and sparks set the house alight. The alarm was raised and most of the family managed to escape – though the eldest son, John, who was blind, had to be helped by servants. The seventy-year-old Major Watson rushed to a second-floor bedroom to attempt to rescue two of his daughters, Elizabeth (twenty-two) and Marion (sixteen), but all three succumbed to the smoke and burned to death. By morning the house was destroyed, with only the fireplaces remaining.

On 23 August 1839, at 6 p.m., a match factory on Woolster Street burst into flames. For the partners, who would go on to become the famous match-making business Bryant and May, this first endeavour obviously proved to be a short-term venture, as by 7.40 p.m. the roof had caved in, and the fire was spreading towards the nearby custom's warehouses of bonded spirits – threatening a major explosion. To add to the danger, the match factory also contained stores of gunpowder. Fortunately, however, fire engines from around the city, including the Royal Dockyard, hurried to the scene, quenching the flames and leaving the premises a pile of smoking ashes.

The Plymouth Slums

In 1832 the terrible sanitary conditions in Plymouth brought on a cholera epidemic that killed 1,031 people. The Plymouth Board of Health desperately tried to control it and the mayor ordered streets to be flushed with water on alternate days. 'Station' houses were established throughout the city to provide blankets, fuel and medicine to victims. The Ford Park Cemetery opened in 1848, and within months a further 400 cholera victims were buried there.

After the castle at the Barbican was demolished, the area was rebuilt into many tiny houses that soon became overcrowded and dilapidated. One survey recorded 564 people living in 30 houses, 13 with no sanitary facilities. By 1850, Castle Street – or Damnation Alley, as it was better known – was a filthy slum noted for debauchery, over a dozen of the thirty houses turned into notorious brothels. A Government report in 1852 suggested the conditions were the worst in Europe, with the exception of Warsaw.

Concern for the moral welfare of the area led to the building of the Bethel Chapel on

Castle Street in 1833, which is now the Barbican Theatre. St Saviour's church was built on the top of Lambhay Hill, though it was later destroyed by the bombing in the Second World War. But the debauchery simply moved west, to the Octagon, where, in 1861, the ironically named James and Louisa Churchward were committed for nine months' hard labour for running a house of ill-repute. This ordinary residential home provided round-the-clock services to the local residents, with women sitting in the windows beckoning in prospective customers and male clientele coming and going at all hours. Their neighbour, John Risdon, recounted how the Churchwards' two adult daughters contributed to their parents' income through prostitution. Their houses were separated only by a thin plaster partition, so he could hear everything that was going on. Despite being threatened with violence by the Churchwards on more than one occasion, he was so revolted by their behaviour that he stood by his front door with a lantern and shone it in the faces of their clients as they left.

The New Palace

The New Palace Theatre on Union Street, now sadly derelict, first opened its doors on 5 September 1898. With sumptuous stage boxes, stalls, grand circle and gallery, it could seat around 2,500 people. Sadly, just four months later it was devastated by fire, and had to be restored and re-opened. It is known to be haunted by an actress, and also a woman called Mary, thought to have died in the fire. A security guard in the 1980s had a terrifying experience whilst patrolling the building with a colleague: at about 3 a.m., the two men heard a woman scream – and all the lights went out.

Mrs Hunn was the mother of the Prime Minister George Canning and an actress. While performing at the New Palace Theatre, she found digs in Plymouth, in a first-floor flat above what had once been a carpenters' workshop. Every night she could hear the sounds of the ghostly carpenters still hard at work, sawing and hammering, even though there was no one downstairs and the door to the street was locked. She mentioned it to the theatre manager, who told her she should leave the flat. Mrs Hunn replied, rather stoically, that the noises didn't worry her – she was more concerned that the noises might stop and the hard-working spirits decide to rest and come upstairs!

In 1908 another tragedy occurred involving a Plymouth theatre, when fifteen-year-old Clara Jane Hannaford had her throat cut just outside the old Theatre Royal by her nineteen-year-old stalker. The

---

Private William Laskey was murdered as he slept in 1877. He had gone to bed intoxicated, and there Corporal Joseph Hector and Private John Mutter attacked him. They kicked and punched him, causing such serious injuries that he died. Others in the room were threatened with the same treatment if they gave the alarm. At the Exeter Assizes the murderers were found guilty of manslaughter and given twelve months' hard labour.

---

obsessed murderer, Edmund Walter Elliott, had followed Clara and her boyfriend to the old theatre. There he called Clara out into the street – where he pulled out a razor and slit her throat. Edmund gave himself up, but calls for clemency on account of his youth were ignored. He was hanged in March 1909.

On 28 April 1912, the *Lapland* arrived in Plymouth carrying 167 survivors of the sinking of the RMS *Titanic*. The 'unsinkable' *Titanic* sank on her maiden voyage after being holed by an iceberg, with 1,517 lives lost in the freezing North Atlantic waters. The *Lapland* anchored in Cawsand Bay, and the passengers were slowly transferred to the *Sir Richard Grenville*, which was supposed to bring the survivors ashore at Millbay Dock. However, the Board of Trade delayed disembarking the passengers until each had been served with a subpoena requiring them to give evidence to the Receiver of Wrecks at Plymouth. Millbay Dock was closed off, guarded by police to prevent any passengers from leaving, but the furious survivors rebelled, refusing to give any evidence at all until their illegal detention was lifted.

Titanic launching – a haunting shot of a boat that would take most of its passengers with it to the depths of the ocean. The few survivors who sailed into Plymouth were not best pleased with their reception... (LC-USZ62-34781)

AD 1914-1918

A WAR TO END ALL WARS

BRITAIN DECLARED WAR on Germany on 4 August 1914, and the workforce at the Devonport dockyards immediately doubled. Around 9,000 extra men and women worked on building new ships, including the Q-ships designed to attack the German's U-boats and testing the new K-class submarines. Submarine K6's trial was disastrous, as the vessel submerged in the Sound and then refused to rise from the seafloor for two hours. The defect was repaired eventually by the inspector of engine-fitters, who was fortunately aboard, but the yard men from Devonport refused to go down in a submarine again.

At the outbreak of war, Salisbury Road Elemental School, like many other schools, became a temporary hospital. All the desks were unscrewed from the floors and replaced by 280 beds, a treatment centre and a neurological department. Less than a month later, the first 100 British and German casualties arrived from northern France.

The greatest early disaster for Plymouth was the loss of the Devonport-built and manned HMS *Monmouth* in the Battle of Coronel, lost off the coast of Chile with no survivors.

At the Battle of Jutland in May 1916 the Royal Navy lost 14 ships and 6,274 men. Five of the lost ships and four of those badly damaged were Devonport-manned. The *Indefatigable* was sunk with only two survivors. The Devonport-built the *Royal Oak*, a 27,500-ton battleship, survived the battle and continued to be deployed until the beginning of the Second World War.

The Royal Oak. *(LC-DIG-ggbain-29189)*

All major roads into Plymouth were heavily guarded against spies and saboteurs. By 1916 there were genuine fears that Plymouth would suffer aerial bombardment from German Zeppelins operating from bases in North-West Europe – and one alarm, fortunately false, brought the town to a standstill. An unidentified naval plane flew over the coast bringing the evening rush hour to a halt. Crowds of residents remained trapped in the streets and in the train stations for several hours before it was revealed that the plane was 'one of ours'.

Meanwhile, soldiers from the Devonshire Regiment were battling in Europe, many of their recruits from Plymouth and most enlisted in Plymouth or Devonport. Atkinson's *The Devonshire Regiment, 1914-1918* is a remarkable book. Tragically, however, over half of its 742 pages are made up of lists of the dead: in the 1st Battalion alone, over 2,600 men died, 291 of them officers.

In 1917 the Devonshire Regiment faced a formidable German line at La Coulette. The Germans' position was very strong, the ground flat and devoid of cover for 2,000 yards, with wire entangle-

A Zeppelin landing in front of Count Zeppelin, the inventor, and the Crown Prince. Fear of aerial attack brought Plymouth to a standstill in 1916. (LC-USZ62-44993)

ments that were unusually thick and the railway embankments nearby proving to be deadly positions for the flanking fire that was bombarding the Devonshire troops. The German artillery at the rear of this formidable fortress was as yet untouched by the British attempts to bombard it – the British artillery was still far behind the ground forces. Atkinson describes the scene: 'despite these formidable obstacles

---

Amanda Bradfield, just eighteen, was murdered by her mother's lodger, James Honeyands, in 1913. Amanda was married to a naval stoker (serving on the HMS *Monmouth*) when she went for a drink in the Courtenay Arms with Honeyands. They quarrelled. The argument continued into the street outside, where Honeyands pulled out a revolver and shot Amanda twice in the chest. He then tried to kill himself, but the revolver jammed. He was apprehended by passers-by.

Amanda did not die immediately, but lingered in hospital for ten days, on one occasion coughing up one of the bullets. Honeyands was charged with murder and hanged on 12 March 1913.

When the German fleet surrendered in 1918, Sir Francis Drake's famous drum at Buckland Abbey, just outside Plymouth, beat a ghostly tattoo. Sir Francis took the drum with him while circumnavigating the world. Legend says that if ever England is in danger, the drum will sound and Sir Francis Drake will return to defend us.

and fatigue and hardships the battalion had endured of late, the men went forward with the utmost dash. From the first, the Devons fared none too well. The hostile barrage caught them in their assembly positions and inflicted many casualties before they moved.'

However, the Devons made a 'fine effort', capturing the first line of German trenches, and 'for a short time the parties who had succeeded in entering the German trenches looked as if they were going to achieve the impossible'. However, German reinforcements arrived, and within a few hours it was reported that only two officers remained unhurt. The party in the German trenches were under fire and 'barely holding on'. By mid-afternoon, the surviving Devons were digging in only a few feet from their starting point that morning. Over seventy were killed in the fighting, with one hundred and sixty wounded.

At the Battle of Fresnay, eighty-six men and officers were killed – including Captain Leonard Maton, who, having being wounded in previous battles, had been 'retired' to a desk job – but he refused to leave the front line. He was killed with his men on 9 May 1917.

One Plymouth man in the midst of these battles was Sergeant Thomas Henry Britton, who was born in Plymouth and enlisted at Devonport. The 1st battalion of the Devonshire Regiment were sent in to relieve the front line at the Somme – their task was to consolidate the position, rescue the wounded and rebuild the trenches, all under heavy shelling. They bravely fought on for three continuous days under fire, suffering 100 casualties, including Thomas. Every centimetre gained in ground at the Somme cost the British two lives.

Reginald Colwill was with the 2nd Devonshire Battalion in France and describes in detail the horror and the triumphs of their final year in battle. His tone is remarkable for its cool descriptions and also its honesty. He heaps great praise on Major Cope, their leader, but also on the men who braved the battles with fortitude and humour: 'Who can explain the psychology of these men, who could face the extreme probability of death with smiles... It was the men who smiled who did great things.'

In March 1918 the Devons had established a headquarters at Brie, but the Germans were rapidly advancing on the other side of the river. After a failed attempt to bomb the bridge, the Devons were told to hold the bridge at all costs and prevent the Germans crossing the river. Now the Devons were the only force to stop them. But the Germans broke the British battle lines further up the river, at Éterpigny, and suddenly the Devons were forced into a retreat, with the enemy 'hammering on our right flank for all he was worth'.

'E' company were the last to move out, with their Lewis gunners blasting at the oncoming German forces. One gunner had his leg shattered by a shell fragment, but kept on firing to prevent the Germans crossing the bridge. For half an hour he stayed at his post, blazing away, firing drum after drum of ammunition into the advancing enemy, taking a 'fiendish delight in watching the deadly effect of his fire', knowing all the while that his company was evacuating its position. This unknown hero not only managed to hold his position, but he even managed to escape and survive the battle.

Suddenly one platoon of 'C' company were entirely surrounded by Germans and had to be left to their fate – it was a tough decision by the commander, but 'it would have been folly to consider throwing men away on merely heroic exploits'.

When 'D' company came under attack, Colwill praised their self-defence: 'God! How they fought... Like demons possessed, they cut and hacked, fighting their way out, inch by inch. In time they succeeded though they left many dead behind them.'

Their next line was near Ablaincourt, facing east. Suddenly there were German soldiers coming over the hills towards them, and 'the troops opened fire and hit a lot of them. Yet, on they came, line followed line... closer and closer every minute.' But 'D' Company was successful in its attack, inflicting an appalling slaughter: 200 German soldiers lay dead in front of them in less than an hour.

Many German transports got stuck on the road, and Colwill describes how four machine-gunners did their work so well that not a single German in the transports was left to tell the tale of what had happened to the rest of them.

GUERRE 1914 - 1917.

The devastation caused at the Front by the new artillery of the twentieth century is shown starkly in this postcard of Arras.

For many months, reinforcements were non-existent and the Devons' forces depleted. On 29 March 1918, at 3 a.m., things looked very bleak for the Devons indeed. The town of Monsel was taken by the Germans, and as the Devons waited for their chance to strike they were appalled by the line of desperate refugees leaving the town, many pushing prams containing sleeping infants, the women crying, going they knew not where. It seemed that nothing could prevent the Germans taking Amiens, and little short of a miracle would save Paris.

At Castel, the German 'barrage was terrible. There was no a gap in it. Machine gun and rifle fire increased in intensity and the wood was full of smoke, flying tree trunks and clouds of earth thrown up by the bursting shells. It was a veritable hell.'

In May 1918, at the Battle of the Bois des Buttes, the 2nd Devons – long since robbed of their regular soldiers through attrition – went down to hopeless odds, with Colonel Anderson-Morshead of the old Plymouth merchant family dying with them, revolver in one hand and hunting crop in the other.

Colonel Anderson-Morshead told the men that their last chance of escape had gone. The bridge ahead of them was taken, the village of Pontavert swarming with the enemy. 'Your job for England, men,' the Colonel said, 'is to hold the blighters up as much as you can, to give our troops a chance on the other side of the river. There is no hope of relief. We have to fight to the last.'

As the commanding officer stoically made his notes with high explosives falling about his ears, less than fifty men managed to survive to cross the river, many dying later of their wounds.

THE FALLEN

DESPITE THE 'WAR to end all wars', in 1939 Britain again found itself fighting the Germans. On the night of 20 March 1941, as winter was coming to an end, German bomber groups of the 3rd Air Fleet, flying from captured air fields in Northern France, attacked and destroyed Plymouth city centre. Within twenty-four hours, the aerial assault intensified, and Plymouth became the worst blitzed city of its size in the UK. Plymouth was left a desolate ruin. For Plymouth, the Second World War would be yet another 'end of the world'.

Night after night in March and April 1941 the German bombs rained down, leaving no street untouched, no family unaffected. Whole families were wiped out in an instant. Thousands left Plymouth each night for the safety of the Dartmoor hills, returning again each morning to work. Thousands more were evacuated, but many stayed, huddling terrified in damp and cramped air-raid shelters as each bombing raid took its toll on the city around them. On 22 April 1941 an air-raid shelter behind the Technical School in Devonport received a direct hit. During repairs three bodies were discovered, those of Olive Spracklan, Phyllis Shortman and Edwin Brazier.

The air-raid shelter at Portland Square was just 1.9m high and 1.4m wide;

A young Nazi airman bailed out of his plane during an air raid in 1943 and landed in Lisson Grove in Mutley Plain, where he was captured by Mr Doidge, the warden. The censors kept one element from the press. While leading the fallen airman through Plymouth, Mr Doidge had used an old piece of string to bind the airman's hands. The censors feared the binding of a prisoner of war's hands would cause an international outcry, so carefully kept it quiet.

> Arthur Martin of Peverell was killed instantly in an explosion at Devonport Docks in 1945. He was working as a burner on the aircraft carrier *Atheling*, and had switched on his torch as he prepared to cut a plate. The torch was faulty and was leaking petrol, and a great jet of flame erupted up the side of the ship. Thick pillars of smoke could be seen all over the dockyard as the police and rescue services rushed to the scene.

standing room only for the local families seeking shelter. On 23 April 1941 the shelter took a direct hit and over seventy people lost their lives. The Mary Newman Student Hall of Residence was built close to the site and Plymouth University students have reported feelings of fear and of being watched, ice-cold blasts of air and the sound of disembodied voices.

Running among the explosions and the fires, the City's Civil Defence Corps maintained communications between the ARP Command Posts, co-ordinating rescues and the fire services, who were desperately short of water. The Corps were a brave band of mainly youngsters, boys barely in their teens, dashing from one emergency to another as streets were devastated around them. Children in wartime Plymouth grew up quickly. The home of one of the boys, David Gibbs, just fifteen, received a direct hit. His family were all killed, but he was never told the terrible news; he was out on the streets, delivering official messages, when an exploding bomb killed him too.

Plymothians remained stoic in the midst of the terror and devastation. One man who grew up in Plymouth during the bombing described how his mother always seemed to cope and never to complain – and then one morning she woke up and her hair had gone completely white.

On 28 April 1941 a mass burial was held in Efford Cemetery for the victims of the Blitz. The service was led jointly by the Bishops of Plymouth and Exeter, the Roman Catholic Bishop of Plymouth and representatives of the Salvation Army, and was attended by all the armed services. The *Western Morning News* reported: 'Here, in a setting of beauty and peace, which looks out over a wonderful panorama of the Devon hills, this company of Plymothians who were called upon to make the supreme sacrifice rest together, men, women and children.'

D-Day

In June 1944 Plymouth was one of the principal staging posts for the Normandy landings, the invasion of France that would eventually end the Second World War in Europe. Plymouth Sound was bursting with ships, and the city packed with thousands of uniformed men, many from America, including General Omar Bradley and the 1st US Army, training at nearby Slapton Sands for their attempt to take the French beaches that would be code-named Omaha and Utah. Vast numbers of tanks and guns were stored around the city, and there was the constant buzz of training and preparation.

Within the storage vaults and battlements of Crownhill Fort, originally built

General Omar Bradley, who trained his men for D-Day at Slapton Sands. (LC-DIG-hec-21734)

to defend Plymouth from the French in the 1800s, soldiers from both world wars scrawled their names on the whitewashed walls, poignant reminders of their presence in Plymouth. The Fort became the training ground for many regiments in the 1940s, including the 111th Field Artillery Battalion, comprising US soldiers recruited into the Virginia Army National Guard.

Sergeants J.S. Holmes and W.J. Bateman from the 111th carefully recorded their names on the wall at Crownhill Fort. They would be in Plymouth for a year, training hard in preparation for their role as artillery cover for the 116th regiment, the 'Stonewall Brigade', also from Virginia. The 116th would be in the first waves of soldiers to land at 'Omaha Beach'.

Suddenly, one morning, Plymothians awoke to find the city eerily deserted. All the ships, all the men and their machines were gone. It was 6 June 1944. D-Day.

Holmes and Bateman were at last making their journey to Normandy as part of the vast Allied forces, but the carnage they faced on their arrival is difficult to imagine. Instead of the infantry advancing up the heavily-fortified beaches, the 111th were presented with mayhem and a coastline awash with the dead.

The 116th regiment, for whom they were to provide cover, had been hit the hardest. Over one third – 1,000 men – of the 116th were already dead or wounded in the first wave. The first ten minutes were a disaster. Several companies no longer existed at all, obliterated by the unexpected fire-power of the German forces entrenched in the ridge forts above the beach. Even the Germans were astonished and dismayed by the

---

An unexploded 70kg bomb was discovered in 2010 by builders in Notte Street, a nasty reminder of the bombing raids of the Second World War. The bomb was transported with great care through the city, under police escort, towards Millbay Docks. All the shop frontages had to be cleared in case the bomb accidentally detonated. The bomb was then transferred onto the bomb disposal unit's diving boat and carried to a few miles off Cawsands, where it was exploded in the water. A massive 15ft jet of spray ended the operation.

The entrance to Crownhill Fort.

slaughter they witnessed. The German commander of Widerstandsnest 76, overlooking the beach, made the following report to his headquarters:

At the water's edge at low tide near St Laurent and Vierville, the enemy is in search of cover behind the coastal obstacles. A great many vehicles – among these 10 tanks – stand burning at the beach. The obstacles demolition squads have given up their activity. Debarkation from the landing boats has ceased, the boats keep farther seawards. The fire of our strong points and artillery was well placed and has inflicted considerable casualties among the enemy. A great many wounded and dead lie on the beach.

There were so many dead that there was no room on the beaches for the next waves of infantry to land. In the chaos, the 111th found themselves on the beach and under fire with no artillery. Their amphibious trucks (DUKWs), transporting their brand new 105mm howitzers to the shore, had either been hit by German forces or swamped, sinking in the English Channel. Senior officers of the military forces had been warned that the amphibious transports could not survive the combined weight of artillery and men under those conditions, but the warning had gone unheeded – and suddenly the 111th were effectively useless.

Not to forget the Pacific Theatre – placed in front of St Andrew's church on 11 November 2011 was a memorial to one Plymouth man who died as a prisoner of war in arguably the worst of all war-time atrocities, the *Maros Maru*.

In 1944, to escape the approaching allies, the Japanese prepared to retreat, determined to take all their POWs with them. A small ship, the *Maros Maru*, set out for the coast of Java with 500 POWs and their Japanese guards aboard, with a further 150 POWs, most suffering from diarrhoea and beri beri, collected en route. The POWs were crammed into every available space, with wounded propped up in stairwells and dying men laid out on the deck in the blistering sun. Storms brought high seas and waves washed over the crowded deck. Suddenly the ship's engines failed and they had to call in for repairs at Macassar. The ship remained in dock for forty days, the heat, beri beri and lack of food killing 150 men; the dying, screaming in agony, were refused all relief. The dead were thrown overboard with sand-bags tied to their feet. Only 325 reached Java, emaciated wrecks of men, many driven insane by the horrific conditions.

Liaison could have warned the transports to delay heading for the beach while they were still under fire, but the radios had been damaged by seawater. One of Battery B's DUKWs was struck by a wave and sank while being launched, well before it made it to the beach – Sergeants Holmes and Bateman were in Battery B. Another six DUKWs sank while circling for six hours, waiting for an opportunity to land.

The survivors of the 111th gathered on the shore, under fire and aware that all their training had come to nothing. Suddenly their commander, Lieutenant Colonel Thomas Mullins, announced to his disheartened terrified men: 'To hell with our artillery mission. We've got to be infantrymen now!' He moved along the seawall, urging his soldiers to return fire, only to be fatally wounded by a sniper's bullet – he was dead within hours. Thomas Mullin's image is on the website at www.marylandmilitaryhistory.org in memory of his brave efforts to save his men and continue their mission.

The surviving members of the Virginia National Guard fought their way in small teams up the beach – all plans tossed aside – braving minefields and the German fortifications, their sheer force of will eventually taking Omaha Beach by nightfall. Landings were finally resumed, with

A statue of Sir Francis Drake guards the War Memorial on Plymouth Hoe. The photograph below shows soldiers storming the beaches during D-Day. (NARA, 23-0455M)

another 20,000 reinforcements landing on 7 June. 'D-Day' resulted in nearly 10,000 Allied casualties – actually less than expected. Thirty-nine men of the 111th Field Artillery Battalion who had trained in Plymouth were amongst the dead.

The two men who had written their names so proudly on the walls of Crownhill Fort, Sergeants J.S. Holmes and W.J. Bateman, are not among the list of casualties. I like to think they made it home in one piece, to families and friends in Virginia.

BIBLIOGRAPHY

Books

Atkinson, C. T. (compiled by), *The Devonshire Regiment 1914-1918*, The Devonshire Press, 1926

Baring-Gould, S., *Devonshire Characters and Strange Events*, J. Lane, The Bodley Head, London, 1908

Bracken, C. W., *A History of Plymouth*, S R Publishers Ltd, 1931

Bray, Mrs A. E., *Traditions, legends, superstitions, and sketches of Devonshire on the borders of the Tamar and the Tavy*, J. Murray, London, 1838

Colwill, R. A., *Through Hell to Victory: From Passchendaele to Mons with the 2nd Devons in 1918*, self-published, 1927

Dacre, M., *Devonshire Folk Tales*, The History Press, 2010

Desmond, A. and Moore, J., *Darwin's Sacred Cause*, Penguin, 2009.

Eliot-Drake, Lady, *The Family and Heirs of Sir Francis Drake*, Volume 1, Smith Elder and Co, 1911

Ellms, C., *The Pirates Own Book*, Dover Publications, 1993, re-edited reprint of 1837 original

Fizzard, A. D., *Plympton Priory: A House of Augustinian Canons in South West England in the late Middle Ages*, Koninklijke Brille NV, Leiden, 2007

Fox, E. T., *Pirates of the West Country*, Tempus Publishing, 2007

Gaunt, P., *The Cromwell Gazetteer*, Alan Sutton Publishing, 1987

Gill, C., *The Naval Mutinies of 1797*, Manchester University Press, 1913

Gill, C., *Plymouth: A New History*, Devon Books, 1993
Sutton Harbour, Devon Books, 1997

Goodall, F., *Lost Plymouth*, Birlinn Limited, 2009

Gray, P., *Graverobbers and Body-snatchers in Devon*, Halsgrave House, 2009

Gray, T., *The Devon Almanac*, Mint Press, 2000

Greeves, Dr T., 'Lydford Castle and Its Prison' in *Dartmoor Magazine*, 79, Summer 2005, pp. 8-10

Grenfell Price, A., (ed) *The Explorations of Captain James Cook in the Pacific*, Dover Publications, 1971.

Harley, P., *The Royal Citadel: Home of the 29 Commando Regiment Royal Artillery*

Hart-Davis, A., and Troscianko, E., *Henry Winstanley and the Eddystone Lighthouse*, Sutton Publishing, 2002

Hawkes, J., *Mount Batten Headland: History and Archaeology*, Plymouth City Museum and Art Gallery, 1998

Hesketh, R., *Devon Smugglers*, Bossiney Books, 2007

Hesketh, R., *Plymouth, A Shortish Guide*, Bossiney Books, 2010

Higham, R. (ed), *Security and Defence in South West England before 1800*, Department of History and Archaeology, University of Exeter, 1987

Hippisley Coxe, A. D., *Haunted Britain*, Hutchinson of London, 1973

Holgate, M., *Murder and Crime: Devon*, Tempus Publishing, 2007
Devon Villains, Rogues, Rascals and Reprobates, The History Press, 2010

Hynes, K., *Haunted Plymouth*, The History Press, 2010

Keble Chatterton, E., *King's Cutters and Smugglers 1700-1855*, George Allen and Company, 1912

Mildren, J., *Castles of Devon*, Bossney Books, Cornwall, 1987

Miller, A. C, 'The Impact of the Civil War on Devon and the Decline of the Royalist Cause in the West of England 1644-5' in *Transactions of the Devonshire Association*, Volume 104, 1972
'The Puritan Minister John Syms' in *Devon and Cornwall Notes and Queries*, Volume 33.5, 1975
Sir Richard Grenville of the Civil War, Phillimore and Co, 1979.

Mode, P. G., *The Influence of the Black Death on the English Monasteries*, a dissertation to the Faculty of the Graduate Divinity School, University of Chicago, 1911

Noble, S., *Plymouth's Barbican and Castle*, Plymouth City Council, 2000

Ollier, E., *Cassell's History of the United States*, Cassell, Peter and Galpin, 1874

Peirce, R., *Pirates of Devon and Cornwall*, Shark Cornwall, 2010

Philbrick, N., *Mayflower*, Penguin, 2006

Photiou, P., *Plymouth's Forgotten War – The Great Rebellion 1642-1646*, Arthur Stockwell, 2005

Platt, R., *Smuggling in the British Isles*, The History Press, 2011

Powicke, M., 'The Thirteenth Century: 1216-1307' from Clark, George (ed) *The Oxford History of England*, Second Edition, 1962

Quigley, L., *The Devil Comes to Dartmoor*, The History Press, 2011

Rule, J. and Wells, R., *Crime, Protest and Popular Politics in Southern England 1740-1850*, The Hambledon Press, 1997

Skinner, J., *Did you know: Plymouth, a Miscellany*, Oakridge, 2010

Snetzler, M. F., *Devon Extracts, The London Gazette 1665-1850*, Volume 2: Plymouth 1665-1765, Devon Family History Society, 1989

Spence, J., *Nelson's Avenger*, Bretonside Copy, 2005
The Smugglers of Cawsand Bay, Bretonside Copy, Plymouth, 2007

Tait, D., *Mount Edgcumbe*, Driftwood Coast Publishing, 2009

Treece, M., *No More The Sword*, William Sessions Limited, 2002

Van Der Kiste, J., *A Grim Almanac of Devon*, The History Press, 2008
Plymouth History and Guide, The History Press, 2009
Plymouth Book of Days, The History Press, 2011
More Devon Murders, The History Press, 2011

Wasley, G., *Blitz: An Account of Hitler's Aerial War Over Plymouth in March 1941 and the Events That Followed*, Devon Books, 1991

Watson, J. Y., *The Tendring Hundred in the Olden Time: A Series of Sketches*, 1877, reprinted by Kessinger Publishing in 2008

Waugh, M., *Smuggling in Devon and Cornwall 1700-1850*, Countryside Books, 1991

White, P., *Classic Devon Ghost Stories*, Tor Mark Press, 1996

Whitfield, H. F., *Plymouth and Devonport in Times of War and Peace*, E. Chapple, 1900

Woodward, F. W., 1987, *Citadel*, Devon Books, 1987

Worth, R. N., *Calendar of the Plymouth Municipal Records*, The Plymouth Corporation, 1893

Newspapers
the Standard, January 23, 1894
BBC News Magazine, 2 November 2011

Online resources
I am indebted to the writers and contributors for the following websites and online resources:

www.ancestry.co.uk
Ballads of the Mutiny 1797: www.mustrad.org.uk/articles/mutiny
BBC WW2 People's War: www.bbc.co.uk/history/ww2peopleswar/
British Civil Wars: www.british-civil-wars.co.uk
UK Battlesfields Resource Centre: www.battle-fieldstrust.com/resource-centre/civil-war
British History Online: www.british-history.ac.uk
Devon Heritage: www.devonheritage.org/Places/Plymouth/Plymouth.htm
Devon Online: www.devon-online.com

Devon Perspectives: www.devonperspectives.co.uk
English Heritage: www.english-heritage.org.uk
UK Genealogy Archives: http://uk-genealogy.org.uk/england/Devon
Legendary Dartmoor: www.legendary-dartmoor.co.uk
www.localhistories.org
National Archives online resources: http://www.nationalarchives.gov.uk
National Trust: http://www.nationaltrust.org.uk
Paranormal Database: www.paranormaldatabase.com
www.thepeerage.com
Plymouth Central Library: www.plymouth.gov.uk/localhistory
www.plymouthdata.info
Derek Tait's excellent blog:http://plymouth-localhistory.blogspot.com,
www.wikipedia.com

For anyone interested in reading personal accounts of Plymouth in the Second World War, I highly recommend these BBC sites:

http://www.bbc.co.uk/ww2peopleswar/stories/70/a5145770.shtml
http://www.bbc.co.uk/ww2peopleswar/stories/49/a4398249.shtml
http://www.bbc.co.uk/ww2peopleswar/stories/53/a2050453.shtml